INTRODUCTION

As a kid I loved going to the pool. Actually, I loved water in general. I was raised all over the world, including Japan, Guam, and California. This meant I spent a lot of my time at the beach or in pools. Not long after moving to Oklahoma we got to go the to local pool. It was burning hot and I missed the California beaches, but the pool was great. I went two to three times a week and made a lot of summer friends by the water.

Our pool had two diving boards. The low board was just a few feet above the water, and we would line up to do cannon balls, belly flops, and ninja dives. You may not know what a ninja dive is. Basically, it is what eight year olds who have watched too many kung fu movies do when they are trying to reenact the kicks and flips seen in movies like Crouching Tiger Hidden Dragon, but from a diving board.

The problem with ninja dives from the low dive is you only have a split second to strike a pose, not quite the moves we were going for.

Weeks into the summer we were daring each other to try the high dive. To an eight year old, it was about a million feet tall so none of us would do it. Still, the thought of having all those seconds of free fall to put on a series of legendary aerial acrobatics … it was tempting. Eventually, I had psyched myself up enough to climb the thousands of steps and edge out to the end of the board. I literally crawled out then looked down. Everyone was watching, so I sucked it up and stood. The board twitched and wobbled with each step as bigger kids yelled for me to hurry up. I stood on the edge and felt my stomach heave and then stepped into history.

All of us had been anticipating that moment, and for my eight year old self it was everything I wanted it to be. After that everyone lined up and we never looked back on that low dive.

That is how I feel about this book. It is so exciting. I feel like we have been in a holding pattern for ages to bring this to you.

Back in May of 2011, I started my Genesis Explained series on my site http://DesignsByNicktheGeek.com. I worked to explain the basics of Genesis, and many in the community found those articles very helpful. For several years I would get regular questions about when I would expand on the series and bring a book to the market.

Then in May 2013, Genesis 2.0 came out and I kicked off the Genesis 2.0 Explained series.

Since then I have done a lot more work both in Genesis and out of it. There are several articles I wrote, but much of what I've learned has been set aside, waiting for this book.

So now here we stand, waiting at the top of the high dive. What are you waiting for? Let's dive in.

ABOUT GENESIS EXPLAINED

THIS BOOK COVERS GENESIS 2.5

This includes Genesis 2.5, 2.5.1, 2.5.2, and 2.5.3 which is the latest version at the time this book was completed.

Genesis is a relatively stable framework, so it is not updated constantly, but it does grow and change over time and those changes become available. If you are using an older version of Genesis, some functions and structure may be addressed that are not in your version of Genesis.

In general, it is best to update and there is rarely a problem for existing sites with the update. Historically there have been a few times where there were issues for users such as Genesis 1.4. However, even in those cases the issues were addressed with updates like Genesis 1.4.1 so ideally you should be using the latest code.

As a final note on the version. Genesis 2.6 is being developed and I'm following along closely. There are some changes that will be included in the next version of the book. Everything in this book will apply to Genesis 2.6 but there are some new features that will be available in 2.6, which will be covered in the update to the book. General concepts in this book will make you familiar with the Genesis codebase so that you will also be able to find and use those changes.

THIS BOOK ASSUMES SOME TECHNICAL SKILLS

This book is not for complete beginners. I don't want you to get frustrated because this book assumes a little knowledge. I do my best to break down the big ideas into things everyone can take away, but if you have never even thought about the languages that make up the web, then you may find the learning curve is too steep.

In the book, I talk about PHP, HTML, CSS, and even JavaScript without explaining the basics of those languages. You do need at least a beginner-level understanding of those languages to use this book. The chapter, "Getting Started with Genesis Explained" contains some useful resources to help you learn those languages.

THIS BOOK INCLUDES EXTRA RESOURCES

There is good news with this. I'm including a short chapter on skills you need to customize a theme. You don't need to start as a master, but if you are brand new, then you will find this information helpful as you get started. At the very least, you will get some vocabulary that will help you with the rest of the book. You will also want to check out the resources section to find other tools, books, and sites you can use to get started and lower the learning curve.

Finally, this book is intended to teach how Genesis is organized, what the more technical parts of Genesis do, and how to interact with it on a code level. The goal isn't to teach plugin or theme development, but I've included a bonus section at the back of the book with some chapters to help aspiring theme and plugin developers get started.

Enjoy.

DEDICATION

Many years ago I decided if I ever wrote a book I needed to add an *in memoriam* for one of my professors. Dr. Vernon Purdy was an amazing teacher but even more I was honored that he counted me as a friend. Sadly he passed away far too young and left a big hole.

He may not have taught me how to develop, but he did encourage logic and an analytical mind, even if he pegged me with a few erasers for asking so many questions.

I also feel it is important to remember Charles Clarkson. Back when Genesis first came out and I was making every mistake that could be made, he was patient and helped me to learn the ins and outs of this great framework. He also passed away before this book was finished.

So consider the legacy of these two great men as you read and I hope that legacy will help you to learn like they helped me to learn.

ABOUT THE OSTRAINING BOOK CLUB

Genesis Explained is part of the OSTraining Book Club.

The Book Club gives you access to all of the "Explained" books from OSTraining:

- These books are always up-to-date. Because we self-publish, we can release constant updates.
- These books are active. We don't do long, boring explanations.
- You don't need any experience. The books are suitable even for complete beginners.

Join the OSTraining Book Club today: https://ostraining.com/books.

Use the coupon "**genesisexplained**" to save 35% on your membership.

ABOUT NICK AND THE OSTRAINING TEAM

Nick "the Geek" Croft is a very early adopter of Genesis. He worked in the support forums as a volunteer and eventually as a paid part-timer. He went on to work as a full-time support person for StudioPress before moving on to working as a developer for the people who build Genesis. Even before he literally wrote the book, he wrote the figurative book on Genesis. Nick is also a core contributor to Genesis and has multiple, popular Genesis plugins.

In addition to being a Genesis fan and developer, Nick is a youth pastor at a church in rural, northern Virginia (not to be confused with Northern Virginia which is far from rural).

Nick has a very supportive and understanding wife who puts up with a case of severe workaholism. Nick is also the father of four amazing children who are growing up way too fast. He is struggling to kick his work habit before the kids all leave home.

He is also into all things geeky, so development isn't just a job, it is a passion.

Books are another addiction for Nick, with a 3-5 book a week habit. He is not interested in breaking that habit.

Stephen Burge has split his career between teaching and web development. In 2007, he combined the two by starting to teach web development. His company, OSTraining, now teaches Drupal classes around the world and online. Stephen is originally from England, and now lives in Florida.

This book also would not be possible without the help of the OSTraining team.

WE OFTEN UPDATE THIS BOOK

This is version 1.0 of Genesis Explained. This version was released January 16, 2018.

We aim to keep this book up-to-date, and so regularly release new versions to keep up with changes in WordPress and Genesis.

If you find anything that is out-of-date, please email us at books@ostraining.com. We'll update the book, and to say thank you, we'll provide you with a new copy.

ADVANTAGES AND DISADVANTAGES

We often release updates for this book. Most of the time, frequent updates are wonderful. If WordPress or Genesis makes a change in the morning, we can have a new version of this book available in the afternoon. Most traditional publishers wait years and years before updating their books.

There are two disadvantages to be aware of:

- Page numbers do change. We often add and remove material from the book to reflect changes in WordPress and Genesis.
- There's no index at the back of this book. This is because page numbers do change, and also because our self-publishing platform doesn't have a way to create indexes yet. We hope to find a solution for that soon.

Hopefully, you think that the advantages outweigh the disadvantages. If you have any questions, we're always happy to chat: books@ostraining.com.

ARE YOU AN AUTHOR?

If you enjoy writing about the web, we'd love to talk with you.

Most publishing companies are slow, boring, inflexible and don't pay very well.

Here at OSTraining, we try to be different:

- **Fun**: We use modern publishing tools that make writing books as easy as blogging.
- **Fast**: We move quickly. Some books get written and published in less than a month.
- **Flexible**: It's easy to update your books. If technology changes in the morning, you can update your book by the afternoon.
- **Fair**: Profits from the books are shared 50/50 with the author.

Do you have a topic you'd love to write about? We publish books on almost all web-related topics.

Whether you want to write a short 100-page overview, or a comprehensive 500-page guide, we'd love to hear from you.

Contact us via email: books@ostraining.com.

ARE YOU A TEACHER?

Many schools, colleges and organizations have adopted OSTraining books as a teaching guide.

This book is designed to be a step-by-step guide that students can follow at different speeds. The book can be used for a one-day class, or a longer class over multiple weeks.

If you are interested in teaching Genesis, we'd be delighted to help you with review copies, and all the advice you need.

Please email books@ostraining.com to talk with us.

SPONSOR AN OSTRAINING BOOK

Is your company interested in sponsoring an OSTraining book?

Our books are some of the world's best-selling guides to the software they cover.

People love to read our books and learn about new web design topics.

Why not reach those people? Partner with us to showcase your company to thousands of web developers.

We have partnered with Acquia, Pantheon, Nexcess, GoDaddy, InMotion, GlowHost and Ecwid to provide sponsored training to millions of people.

If you want to learn more, visit https://ostraining.com/sponsor or email us at books@ostraining.com.

THE LEGAL DETAILS

GENESIS EXPLAINED

NICK CROFT

OSTraining

CONTENTS

PART I.

MAIN BODY

CHAPTER 1.

GENESIS EXPLAINED

Before you start using Genesis, let's give you some background on Genesis itself.

By the end of this chapter, you'll know the answer to some key questions about Genesis, including:

- Who started Genesis?
- Who develops Genesis?
- How much does Genesis costs?
- Who uses Genesis?
- Why should you use Genesis?

WHAT IS GENESIS?

Genesis is a theme framework for WordPress. This means that Genesis is not a traditional WordPress theme. You will not use Genesis as the primary theme on your site. Instead, you'll use a child theme that builds on top of Genesis.

Genesis provides a ton of features that makes it much easier for you to build your child themes. The Genesis code is secure and search engine optimized. It comes with features such as multiple layouts, breadcrumbs, pagination and tons of other useful options.

When you use a child theme, you can benefit from all the features of Genesis, but in a safe space where you can add your own customizations.

WHO BUILDS GENESIS?

Nathan Rice launched the original Genesis theme in 2010 and is still the senior developer today.

Genesis was originally created for and sold by http://StudioPress.com, owned by Brian Gardner. Before StudioPress, Brian started the premium theme industry with a theme called "Revolution". He ended up making several other amazing themes before Genesis, and since then has made even more amazing child themes for Genesis.

The company has evolved and grown over the years. StudioPress merged with Copyblogger, LLC, whose famous blog taught many people how to write web-friendly content. Copyblogger was eventually rebranded as Rainmaker, LLC.

I was fortunate enough to start working with the team from the beginning. I worked with them as StudioPress, Copyblogger, and eventually Rainmaker. So, I have a lot of the inside scoop, so to speak.

In addition to the StudioPress team, there is an amazing community of developers who work with Genesis for clients, their personal sites, or as employees for a different company that contribute to the Genesis core.

HOW MUCH DOES GENESIS COST?

Since Brian started selling Revolution, a whole industry has grown up to provide commercial WordPress themes. There are now thousands of themes for sale in hundreds of marketplaces. Prices for those themes are all over the place, with some themes costing even less than $10 and others running over $100.

Genesis currently costs just under $60.

One of the big advantages of Genesis is the commitment to returning customers. After purchasing Genesis or Genesis plus a child theme, there is an automatic discount applied to future theme purchases. This is usually 25%, but at times can be even more.

They also have a one time "Pro Plus" package available for just under $500. This purchase will give you lifetime access to all past, current and future themes. The Pro Plus package includes all the themes made by the StudioPress team, plus themes developed by third party developers.

You can use the purchased themes on as many sites for yourself, your clients, your friends, and anywhere else as you like with no limits. Since I originally purchased Genesis and the Pro Plus, I've used Genesis on scores of sites. So, my cost per site measures in dollars.

WHAT IS THE CURRENT VERSION OF GENESIS?

As of right now, this very second while I'm typing, Genesis is at version 2.5.3.

The first official version of Genesis was 1.0. The developers follow the same version system as the WordPress core, so when they reached 1.9 they moved to 2.0. So, there have been 16 major versions between 1.0 and 2.5.

Genesis 2.0 was the biggest release so far and happened in 2013. This introduced HTML5 support for Genesis and Genesis child themes. There is a big divide in the child themes between the older XHTML themes (before Genesis 2.0) and the newer HTML5 themes (after Genesis 2.0). Fortunately there is a quick way to identify the newer themes. All the themes released after

2.0 use "Pro" in the name. Examples include "Acadmey Pro," "Business Pro," and "Foodie Pro."

Genesis also releases "point" or "hotfix" versions. These address issues in the major version including updates that are required for changes to WordPress itself. These versions increase the third digit in the version number, so three consecutive hotfix versions will look like this: 2.5.1, then 2.5.2 and then 2.5.3.

WHY SHOULD YOU CHOOSE GENESIS?

The single biggest reason to use Genesis is because of how and why it was built.

Genesis follows the WordPress approach of rarely (if ever) introducing breaking changes. Even the oldest child themes still work with the current version of Genesis. This means that you can always take advantage of new WordPress features without breaking your theme.

Genesis has search engine optimized code, but even more importantly, it is aware of other SEO plugins. This allows Genesis to be highly optimized for users, but also makes allowances for people who have a favorite SEO plugin. This makes it one of the most flexible solutions for SEO in the market.

Another great benefit to Genesis is the plethora of available plugins. There are over 70 plugins in the WordPress plugin repository (including several of my own), with even more available outside of the free repository at this moment.

Genesis does not arrive with every feature you will want, but it's highly likely that the feature exists as a plugin or child theme. This means that Genesis can be lean and fast but extendible with exactly the features needed for any given site.

Finally, Genesis is fast. The StudioPress developers recently updated Genesis to add support for some of the most popular caching plugins.

WHO USES GENESIS?

The simple answer to this is, a lot of people use Genesis. According to BuiltWith.com, Genesis is installed on nearly half a million websites.

You can find a detailed list of sites built with Genesis at https://studiopress.com/showcase. Let's give you a brief overview of Genesis sites in a wide range of different industries. You'll see a wide range of designs, illustrating just how flexible Genesis can be.

Education: Alaska Pacific University uses a Genesis-powered site at https://alaskapacific.edu.

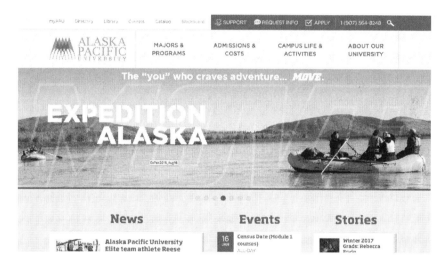

Business: Hutcherson Law are a legal firm based in Dallas, Texas and their Genesis site is at https://hutchersonlaw.com.

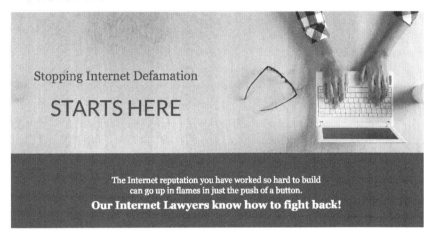

Marketing Professionals: Spears Marketing is a digital agency based in Kentucky, and you'll find their website at https://spearsmarketing.com.

Entertainment: The historic downtown Kalamazoo State Theatre in Michigan is a popular venue for concerts, shows, entertainment, and private events: https://kazoostate.com.

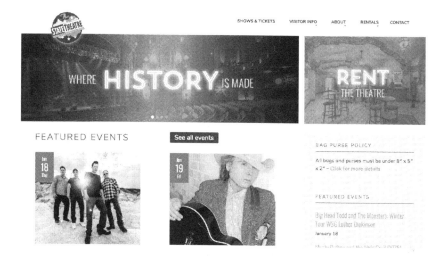

Mom Blogs: The Budget Mom is an Accredited Financial Counselor® based in Spokane, Washington. She helps real women live on a real budget: https://thebudgetmom.com.

Photography Studios: Edward John is a Metro Detroit area photographer who has traveled the world taking photos for weddings: http://edwardjohnphotography.com.

Non-Profits: The Ellen MacArthur Cancer Trust is a registered charity set up with its main aim to help children and young adults aged between 8-24 to regain their confidence through sailing: https://ellenmacarthurcancertrust.org.

WHAT'S NEXT?

Now you have a good idea of what Genesis is and why you would want to use it. Let's start to dive into the Genesis code.

The next several chapters will show you how develop websites with Genesis. You will learn all about Genesis functions, classes, hooks and filers.

In the next chapter, we're going to cover what a framework is and we'll show how how Genesis' structure makes it so flexible.

CHAPTER 2.

GETTING STARTED WITH GENESIS EXPLAINED

In this chapter, you'll get set up to follow along with this book.

We'll show you how to set up a child theme so you can safely make code edits and changes.

We'll also give you an overview of the tools and skills that we recommend in order to successfully follow the book.

SETTING UP A CHILD THEME TO FOLLOW ALONG

Starting in the next chapter, I'm going to ask you to open up some files in the Genesis theme. You will see this warning over and over:

```
WARNING: This file is part of the core Genesis
Framework.
```

Here's a screenshot from the page.php file in Genesis. In fact, this is the entire page.php file!

```
 1   <?php
 2   /**
 3    * Genesis Framework.
 4    *
 5    * WARNING: This file is part of the core Genesis Framework. DO NOT edit this file under any circumstances.
 6    * Please do all modifications in the form of a child theme.
 7    *
 8    * @package Genesis\Templates
 9    * @author  StudioPress
10    * @license GPL-2.0+
11    * @link    http://my.studiopress.com/themes/genesis/
12    */
13
14   // This file handles pages, but only exists for the sake of child theme forward compatibility.
15   genesis();
16
```

You should listen to these warnings! Much of this book is about how you make your own custom theme or plugin without needing to edit the Genesis files.

Step #1. Choose your starting point. You may have purchased a child theme when you purchased Genesis and want to use that as your starting point. Otherwise, you can start with the free Genesis Sample theme from: https://studiopress.com/sample/.

- Download the Genesis framework and install it in your WordPress site.

- Download your child theme or the Genesis Sample theme. Install it into your WordPress site.

It is important that you have both Genesis and the child theme installed, because the child theme will not work without Genesis. The image below shows both Genesis and the child theme installed into the correct folder:

The next image below shows the contents of the /genesis-sample/ folder. Most of your edits will go into the functions.php and style.css files. You may also need to create some template files. Because you will be editing the functions.php file, it is possible a typo or other error can bring your site down. If that ever happens, check out the "How to Recover a Crashed Genesis Site" chapter for some solutions that will bring your site back up.

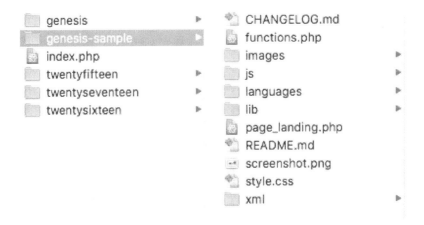

Finally, if you have purchased another child theme like the very popular Academy Pro and Foodie Pro themes, you may be hesitant to edit the child theme. Often people look for a way to create a child theme from the child theme. At this time that is not possible. All edits will go into the child theme. The good news is most updates are intended to be applied to the parent theme, not the child theme. If there is an update to the child theme, it is not usually required that the edit be applied to the site. Should it be a more important security issue (which is very rare in a child theme because of how Genesis is being used as a framework), there are typically instructions on how to apply the update to the child theme. I've only seen this a couple of times in all my time working with Genesis, so it really is exceedingly rare that a child theme must be updated.

Remember:

There are no grandchild themes.

TOOLS YOU'LL NEED

Editing code does not require more than the most basic text

editors. There are developers who use "ancient" tools like Vim and Emacs to create their code, but most developers are interested in an easier experience. Modern development tools like IDEs make for great tools to develop with. This doesn't mean you need to shell out thousands of dollars though. There are free and relatively inexpensive solutions available.

You also need a reasonably modern computer. You can use something from the 90s, but you will be stuck with more ancient editors and will absolutely not have access to modern browsers. This is what the worst limitation is with old equipment. Access to modern browsers makes it significantly easier to develop. All modern browsers, including Microsoft now, include a code inspector. This allows you to look at the HTML, CSS, and even JS and inspect how it works on the site. This allows you to make experimental changes so that you can see how a wider margin will look before you add it to the style sheet.

You will also want access to a local development and remote staging environment.

Local tools like XAMPP (https://apachefriends.org) and MAMP (https://mamp.info) as well as Local by Flywheel (https://local.getflywheel.com) allow you to develop locally before you push your code up to a server. This makes it easier to catch issues and quickly prototype instead of having to upload via FTP or SSH before seeing your changes.

Remote staging servers are a place where you can test your code and let clients or partners see the changes before they go into production. If you have a shared hosting environment, this can be as simple as adding a subdomain for your site like staging.example.com. Then install WordPress and make sure your code gets put up there before it goes into production.

Even better, you may have a host that integrates with Git or a Continuous Integration/Deployment solution so you can use version control while also having integrated Staging and Deploy environments. The is is really the best solution.

In the "Recommended Tools" heading, I offer some more explanation as well as specific tools that you might look at, though there are many other options that will work.

SKILLS YOU'LL NEED

So, you have a nice new theme with tons of features, but you want to make changes so it will be uniquely yours. You are at a crossroad. Do you hire a developer or do you become a developer? There are risks and benefits for both. A skilled developer will know how to accomplish things you never thought possible. They will transform your site into what you want it to be, and it will happen much faster than you could do it yourself. A skilled developer is also an expensive option. Developer rates generally start at $50/hour and run up to $200/hour for this type of development, though some can charge more or less.

This sends many into the "I can do this myself" camp. The most obvious benefit to developing the theme yourself is a potential savings of hundreds of dollars. This is certainly convincing, but be sure to consider the hidden costs. What is your time worth? If you plan on having a great looking and functioning site, you will need to learn CSS, HTML, and enough PHP to understand how to alter the code you find. It is something you can learn, but jumping straight into the deep end isn't advisable.

For all of these topics, check out the coding classes at OSTraining: https://ostraining.com/classes/coding.

Learning HTML

You will need to learn the basics of html, or you won't be able to follow the CSS tutorials or create links, insert images, or much else.

The most important concepts you will want to learn are:

- Divs
- Spans
- Anchors (links)
- Images
- Headings
- Paragraphs
- Breaks
- Lists

There are many other HTML elements, but if you can learn the ins and outs of these ,you will have a good foundation for moving forward.

Learning CSS

Once you have a firm foundation in HTML, you will want to understand how to make it look pretty. HTML without CSS is bland at best. CSS controls, size, color, background, layout, and pretty much every visual component of your site.

There is much to learn about CSS before you are a black belt, but if you can get the basics down you can get started with WordPress theme development. Be sure to learn:

- Backgrounds
- Color
- Fonts
- Padding

- Border

- Margin

- Floats

Again, there is a lot more to CSS than that, but if you are proficient in these concepts, you can search for the rest of the answers pretty easily.

Learning PHP

This is the single most difficult thing you will need to learn. PHP is about logic construction. It is unlikely you will need to learn enough PHP to actually create anything, but you will need to learn enough to alter the code you find in tutorials, and this means understanding what is happening.

You will want to have a pretty good grasp of these concepts:

- Strings

- Arrays

- Comments

- Variables

- If…Else

- Loops

- Functions

If you can learn this, then you should be able follow most of what the code is doing and how to adapt it to your unique needs.

RECOMMENDED TOOLS

Developers all have their preferred tools. Many use very expensive software to make their jobs easier. If you are trying to save money, you probably want software in the inexpensive to free range. Fortunately there are a lot of great tools available for little to nothing. In fact, every tool I will recommend here is free.

FTP Tools

You really need to learn how to access your site via FTP. Even if you do most of your editing in the WordPress editor, you will need FTP in case you break the theme and can no longer access your site. A few good FTP programs include:

- **FileZilla**: Available on all major OS, including Linux
- **Cyberduck**: Mac-specific
- **WinSCP**: Windows specific
- **FireFTP**: FireFox FTP extension

Code Editor

File editors fall into a couple of categories. At the most basic level, you have plain text editors. Pretty much all operating systems come with some kind of plain text editor such as "Notepad" for Windows. You can open any web document in one of these editors, and this may be all you need. However, there are extended text editors available that will markup your text, set tabs, and even check for errors. Some will even connect via FTP to automatically update your files. A few include:

- **Notepad++**
- **NetBeans**
- **Coda2**
- **PHPStorm**

Image Editor

Most folks are familiar with Adobe Photoshop. This is very expensive software, but you can get most of the features with

Photoshop Elements. Still I said I would be recommending free programs, so if you are on a shoestring budget, check out Gimp. This is a free image editor that can be extended via free scripts and plugins into a very powerful image editor to rival Photoshop. It can also open Photoshop (PSD) files. If you need to work with vector art, you can use Inkscape which works with Illustrator files.

Another great tool for designing webpages is Sketch. It has a lot of tools that make it easy to build, starting with wireframes then moving on to creating assets, modules, and generating a web page visually before generating the assets and developing the site.

Additional Tools

There are two other very important tools you need.

Browser tools for Chrome, Firefox or Safari. These are a developers best friend. It can help you identify which CSS definition is affecting a given element and lets you test changes to a live site, though you still need to add the changes to your stylesheet to make it a permanent change. Firefox has a lot of built-in functions you are unlikely to need, but it's great to have them if you ever need them. Safari and Chrome also have a built-in developer tool set you can use. Internet Explorer has also jumped on the developer tools bandwagon. It is not as advanced as Chrome or FireBug, but you can use FireBug Lite to access some of the features from Firefox.

W3C Markup Validation Service. This is an online web resource at https://validator.w3.org. It will validate your website for proper HTML. Many errors between browsers are not actually CSS related, but improper validation. Run your site through this validator and then resolve the errors.

RECOMMENDED DEVELOPERS

After reading this, you may decide that spending countless hours learning HTML, CSS and programming could be better spent creating your site's content and that you would like to expedite your website's launch. If so, it is worth the investment to hire a skilled developer from StudioPress' recommended developers: http://studiopress.com/genesis-developers.

CHAPTER 3.

THE GENESIS FRAMEWORK EXPLAINED

Genesis does have a learning curve and some developers can become frustrated when they start working on the framework.

I know this is true, because I did everything wrong when I first started with Genesis.

I can remember my very first client for Genesis. He had read an article about the framework and wanted to use it for his site. I went out and bought a license then started modifying the Genesis theme directly. This was back in the days of Genesis 1.0 and there weren't huge warnings against that as there are now. I didn't get the hype about Genesis and nothing seemed to work right. I finally got the project done. It was only then I read the documentation and realized that I'd done everything wrong.

I had to spend the next week learning how to work with Genesis correctly, and then another week re-doing all my work for the client.

The whole process made me angry. I didn't start to appreciate Genesis until I stopped treating it like a traditional theme.

In a regular theme, you start by duplicating key files. For example, you may look for a single.php, page.php or index.php to start customizing single post pages. In Genesis, most of these files don't exist, or if they do exist, they have a single line of code:

```php
<?php
genesis();
```

In your child theme, there may only be a style.css and functions.php file. The functions.php may only have a single line of code in it. From this tiny bit of coding, there are huge changes in the look and feel of the theme, but very little for developers to copy and modify.

This system actually allows for much more efficient coding, but only when the basic concepts are clearly understood. This book will explain how all of this works to make your life easier.

UNDERSTANDING THE FRAMEWORK

Genesis is a framework. You can think of it like Lego or a similar toy. Genesis is a platform that other pieces fit onto, and those pieces can be removed or moved. Like Lego, some pieces have to fit in specific places, while you can add other pieces almost anywhere.

The basic platform cannot be altered though, so lets look at that platform.

```php
<?php
/**
 * Genesis Framework.
 *
 * WARNING: This file is part of the core
Genesis Framework. DO NOT edit this file under
any circumstances.
 * Please do all modifications in the form of a
child theme.
 *
```

```
 * @package Genesis\Framework
 * @author   StudioPress
 * @license GPL-2.0+
 * @link     http://my.studiopress.com/themes/
genesis/
 */

/**
 * Used to initialize the framework in the
various template files.
 *
 * It pulls in all the necessary components
like header and footer, the basic
 * markup structure, and hooks.
 *
 * @since 1.3.0
 */
function genesis() {

    get_header();

    do_action(
'genesis_before_content_sidebar_wrap' );

    genesis_markup( array(
        'open'    => '<div %s>',
        'context' => 'content-sidebar-wrap',
    ) );

        do_action( 'genesis_before_content' );
        genesis_markup( array(
            'open'    => '<main %s>',
            'context' => 'content',
        ) );
            do_action( 'genesis_before_loop' );
```

```
        do_action( 'genesis_loop' );
        do_action( 'genesis_after_loop' );
    genesis_markup( array(
        'close' => '</main>', // End .content.
        'context' => 'content',
    ) );
    do_action( 'genesis_after_content' );

genesis_markup( array(
    'close'   => '</div>',
    'context' => 'content-sidebar-wrap',
) );

do_action(
'genesis_after_content_sidebar_wrap' );

get_footer();

}
```

This is the framework.php file, one of three files that are essentially unalterable. Let's look at it closer.

Immediately you will notice there is a "warning" in the code that says the file should not be edited. In fact, you should not edit any core Genesis file. Any changes will be undone if you upgrade Gensis. Instead, you should do all work via a child theme.

Scroll down to line 22, which reads "**function** genesis() {". Here is where the action starts.

The "function genesis() {" is invoked in nearly every standard template file. It loads this code.

At the top and bottom should be two familiar functions, "get_header()"and "get_footer()". They load the header.php file and footer.php file. Those are the other two files that can't really be changed because they make up the core platform of the framework.

Within the header and footer, there is an HTML structure, as well as "do_action()" functions. These are the "hooks" that actions are attached to. In other words, they are the little bumps that the other Lego pieces attach to.

This file has seven hooks, but some of those will have hooks loaded onto them, depending on what functions are being added by actions. I'll be explaining actions later, but for now I'll simplify this by showing the typical hook structure.

Here is a simplified reference in the order the hooks load, starting with the hooks that load the actual framework:

Init.php

- genesis_pre
- genesis_pre_framework
- genesis_init
- genesis_setup

Header.php

- genesis_doctype
- genesis_title
- genesis_meta
- genesis_before
- genesis_before_header
- genesis_header

    ◦ genesis_site_title

- ◦ genesis_site_description
- ◦ genesis_header_right
- • genesis_after_header

Framework.php

- • genesis_before_content_sidebar_wrap
  - ◦ genesis_before_content
    - ▪ genesis_before_loop
      - ▪ genesis_loop

        HTML5
        - ▪ genesis_before_entry
          - ▪ genesis_entry_header
          - ▪ genesis_before_entry_content
            - ▪ genesis_entry_content
          - ▪ genesis_after_entry_content
          - ▪ genesis_entry_footer
        - ▪ genesis_after_entry

        XHTML
        - ▪ genesis_before_post
          - ▪ genesis_before_post_title
            - ▪ genesis_post_title
          - ▪ genesis_after_post_title
          - ▪ genesis_before_post_content

- genesis_post_content
  - genesis_after_post_content
- genesis_after_post

Comments.php

- genesis_before_comments
- genesis_comments
  - genesis_list_comments
    - genesis_before_comment
    - genesis_after_comment
    - genesis_before_comment
    - genesis_after_comment
- genesis_after_comments
- genesis_before_pings
- genesis_pings
  - genesis_list_pings
    - genesis_before_comment
    - genesis_after_comment
    - genesis_before_comment
    - genesis_after_comment
- genesis_after_pings
- genesis_before_comment_form
- genesis_comment_form
- genesis_after_comment_form

- genesis_after_endwhile
- genesis_loop_else
- genesis_after_loop
- genesis_after_content

Sidebar.php

- genesis_before_sidebar_widget_area
  - genesis_sidebar
- genesis_after_sidebar_widget_area
- genesis_after_content_sidebar_wrap

Sidebar-alt.php

- genesis_before_sidebar_alt_widget_area
  - genesis_sidebar_alt
- genesis_after_sidebar_alt_widget_area

Footer.php

- genesis_before_footer
  - genesis_footer
- genesis_after_footer
- genesis_after

Wow, that's a lot of hooks! There are additional hooks run in the admin side of Genesis as well, which I will discuss in the Admin section of this book.

Each one of these hooks can have additional functions added, which are typically just a few lines of code that can move entire sections of the site around.

GENESIS STYLE SHEET BASICS

Back in the 1980s my parents bought a Commodore 64. If you were born after 1985, you may not know what this is. Shoot, even if you were born before that you may not. In short, it was an old computer. This was years before the first Windows PC came out. I remember learning to play games on it and wanting to modify them. It got me on track to become the geek I am today.

A few years later, the internet began to take off. Back then you built websites in pure HTML. It was complicated to make changes across the site because you had to go and change all the parts that defined it. Then CSS came out and created a solution for styling a webpage.

Modern web development takes it for granted because it's been here since **almost** the beginning.

A lot of people worry about styling because it requires very specific formatting, but CSS isn't really that difficult to learn. The bonus section includes a bit more info on how it works, plus some references that you can use to really dig in.

Genesis and most WordPress themes rely on a single file called style.css which contains many of the most important CSS elements. In the Genesis version of style.css, you will find a bunch of rules that look something like this:

```
body,
h1,
h2,
h2 a,
h2 a:visited,
h3,
```

```
h4,
h5,
h6,
p,
select,
textarea {
    color: #333;
    font-family: "Helvetica Neue", Arial,
Helvetica, sans-serif;
    font-size: 16px;
    font-weight: 300;
    line-height: 1.5625;
    margin: 0;
    padding: 0;
    text-decoration: none;
}
```

The list from "body" to "textarea" are called "selectors".

Selectors are created using listing HTML tags, with the following formatting:

- Classes use a "." before the class name, like ".class-name".
- IDs use a "#" before the ID, like "#ID-name".
- Or, you can use a combination.

Items on the same tag element must be joined together without a space.

```
<div class="class-name second-class"></div>
```

This could be targeted using any of these selectors:

```
.class-name {

}
```

```
.second-class {

}

div.class-name {

}

div.second-class {

}

div.class-name.second-class {

}
```

Nested elements are specified with a space in the order that the elements are nested.

```
<div class="class-name">
<p class="nested-item"></p>
</div>
```

The "p" element here may be targeted with any of these selectors:

```
p {

}

.nested-item {

}

p.nested-item {
```

```
}

div p {

}

.class-name .nested-item {

}

.class-name p {

}

div.class-name p {

}

div .nested-item {

}

div.class-name p.nested-item {

}
```

The concept behind CSS is that rules can be replaced, so you can have some rules for "p" tags, but other rules for "p" tags inside a container with the class "class-name". You can have other, even more specific rules for a tag with the class "nested-item" within another class "class-name."

This is extremely useful in a dynamic environment when users might be placing different widgets into the same sidebar, or choosing from a wide variety of layouts that will need slightly different styling.

One last note on selectors. There are a few other selectors that you can use, including attributes and psuedoclasses. Some browsers have difficulty with the more advanced selectors, so if you need to support older browsers, be cautious.

In addition to selectors, there are the actual declarations. These are two part statements that tell the browser what to do with the elements defined by the selectors. They belong inside the brackets. So you would have:

```
selector {
property: value; /*this line is a declaration*/
}
```

There are a few common mistakes I see people making. Using broken syntax or values that don't exist seem to be the most likely errors. Broken syntax can fall into a pretty wide range of possible errors. The most common is missing terminators.

These can be a real beast to find. Dropping the closing "}" or the ";" can break things pretty bad.

```
selector {
property: value /*note the missing ;*/
property-two: value-two; /* neither of these
declarations will work because the previous
doesn't "end" till this ; stops it, so now the
value isn't valid */
}

selector {
property: value;

/* without the closing } nothing will work
right after this line */
```

Remember: Always add your CSS edits to the child theme, just like with PHP, no edits should be added to the Genesis theme.

WHAT'S NEXT?

Now you are starting to get an understanding of what Genesis is. Unlike many other themes, Genesis intended to be worked with by child themes and plugins exclusively. This adds a lot of great benefits, but it does mean that Genesis has a bit of a learning curve. This book will get you to the top of the curve.

The next chapter is about actions. These are the core components that add almost everything that appears on the front end of a Genesis site, so it is important to start there. When you master actions, most other concepts will start falling into place. After the actions, I'll explain how to read the Genesis files to learn how to quickly find the right code to copy into your theme for editing.

If you still feel a little lost, don't worry too much. Each step in this book will help explain the framework more clearly, but this foundation will also make it easier to understand the next chapter.

CHAPTER 4.

GENESIS ACTIONS EXPLAINED

In the previous chapter, I explained how Genesis is a framework that is not dissimilar from working with Lego.

We saw all the built-in hooks in Genesis. We made the Lego analogy that these hooks are like the bumps that let you attach bricks to each other.

Continuing the Lego comparison, if the hooks are those bumps, the actions are the instructions that show where a brick should be placed. The Lego brick itself is a piece of code called a function.

There are two basic kinds of actions, "add_action()" and "remove_action()". They do exactly what the name says they do.

- An "add_action()" is an instruction on where to add a brick (function).
- A "remove_action()" is an instruction to remove the piece of code.

There are five parts to the instruction.

1. **Instruction Type**: This is going to be "add" or "remove".
2. **The Hook to be Used**: This is where the code goes.

3. **The Call Back Function**: This is the code that will be added.
4. **The Priority**: This shows what order the code is loaded relative to other actions.
5. **Accepted Args**: This is the number of variables that can be sent to the function.

Those are the principles we'll be using in this chapter as we explore action. Lets see how these principles work with the Genesis codebase.

ADD ACTION

Here is a generic add action:

```
add_action( 'hook', 'callback_function', 10, 1 );
```

Let's look at the five parts of the instruction in more detail.

1. Instruction Type

The first part of the instruction tells us it is adding an action, not removing one.

2. The Hook to be Used

The second part of the action tells us the hook's name is "hook". If this hook doesn't exist, then the code doesn't do anything else. This is helpful since you don't need to deal with conditional code to make sure the hook exists.

It also means you don't need to worry about your function loading if the hooks haven't loaded. This is used in Genesis for the loop and comment template. If the loop isn't loaded, then the remaining loop hooks don't load. Likewise, if the comment template isn't loaded, then none of the other comment hooks load.

3. The Callback Function

The third part tells us the name of the callback function is "callback_function". This must exist, or you will get an error to the effect of "The second argument is expected to be a valid callback function." This message means you must either use an existing function, or you need to create a function.

All you need to do is write this in a PHP file that will be loaded when this action is executed (typically just before or after the action code).

```php
function callback_function() {

//do something really cool

}
```

- The first part says "Hey, this is a function for you to remember."
- The next part is the function name.
- Inside the () would be any arguments that can be passed (more on that later).
- The { is the start of the function.
- Everything after that is code that runs inside the function.
- The } is the end of the function.

This is relatively simple code, but also very easy to mess up. Misspell any of that, use the wrong symbol, or put something out of order, and you will get an error. Learn to read those errors, and you will know how to fix it, but that's another chapter. The short version is, type it out like this, and you won't break anything.

4. The Priority

The fourth part is the priority. In this case it is "10," which is the default. If this number is not set, then WordPress will see it as a 10. Any actions with the same priority will get loaded in the order the code occurs which is typically:

- WordPress core functions
- Most plugins
- Framework files
- Theme function files
- Theme template file

This isn't 100% true in all cases because of the way some actions are added. However, the important take away is if you find something loading in the wrong order, this number can be adjusted to control when it appears relative to other actions.

The lower the number, the higher the priority. Or, in other words, the actions with the lowest numbers will load first. This means you can put several items on the same hook and use priority to force them into the exact order you want.

```
add_action( 'hook', 'function_1'     ); //loads
second

add_action( 'hook', 'function_2', 15 ); //loads
last

add_action( 'hook', 'function_3', 5  ); //loads
first
```

Notice none of these have the arguments (which we will talk about next), and only the second two use the priority. The first defaults to "10," so it comes between the second and third.

5. Accepted Args

The fifth part is the accepted args. This defaults to "1," but you don't have to actually pass any args along. Normally this is left at 1, since the actions aren't actually passing along anything that can be used. However, there are times when this can be very useful. In my plugin, "Genesis Featured Widget Amplified," I get my "$instance" value for the widget settings and send that outside the class via the hook function. This means I can write code in my functions.php file and have it check the widget settings before it does anything.

```php
add_action( 'gfwa_post_content',
'gfwa_do_post_content', 10, 1 );
/**
 * Outputs the selected content option if any
 *
 * @author Nick Croft
 * @since 0.1
 * @version 0.2
 * @param array $instance Values set in widget
instance
 */
function gfwa_do_post_content( $instance ) {

    if ( !empty( $instance['show_content'] ) ) {

        if ( $instance['show_content'] ==
'excerpt' ) {

            the_excerpt();

        } elseif { ( $instance['show_content']
== 'content-limit' )

            the_content_limit( ( int )
```

```
$instance['content_limit'], esc_html(
$instance['more_text'] ) );

    } else {

        the_content( esc_html(
$instance['more_text'] ) );

    }
  }
}
```

This code checks the "$instance" value to see if this should show "the_excerpt()", "the_content_limit()", "the_content()", or do nothing at all. If you didn't see that, the important part is that I added the "$instance" value as an argument. Since we don't work with this very often in actions, I'll move on for now, and deal with this in depth when I explain filters.

Duplicate Actions

The last thing you need to know is duplicate "add_actions" are ignored. If an action exactly matches, it will do nothing. If any part is different, including the priority or accepted arguments, then it will load onto the site again.

```
add_action( 'hook', 'function_1' );
add_action( 'hook', 'function_1' ); //this is
ignored since that instruction already exists
add_action( 'hook', 'function_1' ,5 ); //this
will load before the first instance of
function_1() on "hook"
add_action( 'hook_2', 'function_1' ); //this
will load the code in function_1() onto "hook_2"
```

In the first part of this chapter, you've seen how to add an action by writing a simple instruction that says where to put it, what to put there, what order to put it in and any special parts the code might need. The next step is learning how to remove the action.

REMOVE ACTION

A remove action has all the same parts. The biggest difference is the remove action depends on an add action and hook, not just the hook. Remember that the "add_action()" is ignored if the hook isn't present. Well, the "remove_action()" won't do anything if the corresponding "add_action()" isn't present. Lets try some examples ...

```
add_action( 'hook', 'function_1'    );
add_action( 'hook', 'function_1', 5 );

remove_action( 'hook', 'function_1' );
remove_action( 'hook', 'function_2' );
```

Here we have two "add_action()" lines. Both load the same function, but in a different priority. I've also added two "remove_action()" lines.

The first "remove_action()" will remove the first "add_action" but ignore the second, even though it uses the same hook and function. Because the remove action is not exactly the same, including any priority or accepted argument values, it will not remove that specific action.

The second "remove_action()" does nothing in this case. It doesn't have an action that it matches because the actions are using different functions. If any part of the add action is not an exact match, then the remove action does nothing. It will not return an error though. This is useful if an action is only added conditionally, but you don't want to build the same conditional contingency for removing the action.

For example, removing a portion of the comment form can be done without making sure you are on a single page first, even though the form only loads on single pages.

There is one other caveat. The "add_action" has to exist before the "remove_action".

```
remove_action( 'hook', 'function_3' );
add_action(    'hook', 'function_3' );
```

This will still load the action because it is added after the remove action has said "now take off this piece."

In sum, if the "remove_action" exactly matches the "add_action" and comes after the "add_action", then it will tell WordPress to remove that bit of code.

ACTIONS IN LOOPS

If that last rule of "remove_actions" seems unfair, this is why it exists. Take a look at the "Changing the Gallery Post Format Output" section in the "Code Reference" chapter of the Appendix. A summary of that code is explained below.

If you notice, the code is added inside the loop ("genesis_before_post" is the first hook in the loop). This means it is repeated every time a new post is loaded in the loop. Based on what we know about actions, the duplicate "add_action" lines are ignored. If the action has already been removed, the "remove_action" will do nothing. Since this code deals with two different scenarios, which might change, the actions need to be added/removed every time.

```
//within the loop

if( $foo == $bar ){
```

```
add_action(    'hook'  , 'function_1' );
remove_action( 'hook_2', 'function_1' );


}

else {

add_action(    'hook_2', 'function_1' );
remove_action( 'hook'  , 'function_1' );


}
```

In this example, we are assuming the code is looped and that the "$foo" and "$bar" variables change. So they might be equal at times and not equal at other times, which is why I have two options. If the first condition is true, then I am adding the code to hook, but I don't want the code to show on "hook_2", so I have to remove it, even if the code wasn't added. In the second condition, the first not being true, then I add the code to "hook_2" but have to remove it from the hook because it may or may not have been added previously.

Because identical actions are not duplicated, and because "remove_actions" depend on the "add_action" already existing, this lets me use very simple code to move my function from one hook to the other in a loop.

WHAT'S NEXT?

This chapter has introduced the principles behind actions in Genesis.

Now you will need to apply your new knowledge. The next chapter explains how to find actions in the Genesis files and alter them within the child theme. This is the number one way to quickly alter the layout of a page. With these skills you will be able to rearrange entire sections of a page.

CHAPTER 5.

GENESIS FRAMEWORK ACTIONS EXPLAINED

In the chapter, "The Genesis Framework Explained," I gave a general introduction to how the Framework works. We saw the contents of a single file to show how hooks are used in the framework.

In "Genesis Actions Explained," I explained how add/remove actions work and the technical rules around them.

Now, I'm going to tie these two ideas together, bridging the gap between the theoretical actions and the framework.

THE DIRECTORY STRUCTURE

Let's start by talking files.

Genesis does a great job of using directory structure to organize files. Here is the directory structure found in Genesis, with a very brief description of what the files within the directory do:

- **genesis**: Contains all files and directories. The files exposed in this directory are general template files, mostly loading other files in the framework. The header.php and footer.php are core framework files with hooks.

  ○ **images**: This has all the images used with the Genesis

theme. Since you should be using a child theme, this doesn't do much.

- **lib**: Holds the core files for the Framework. The init.php file loads all the other files, and the framework.php file contains the core hooks used by the framework.

  - **admin**: Includes files related to admin operations.

  - **classes**: Contains files with php classes used by the theme.

  - **css**: Loads styles for the admin section of the site.

  - **function**s: This contains the general or helper functions used in the theme and child themes.

  - **js**: Handles script loading for the theme, includes admin, comment, and menu scripts.

  - **languages**: Handles translation files.

  - **shortcodes**: This has all the short codes built into the theme.

  - **structure**: Handles the output on the front end of the site, the remainder of this section will be dealing with this directory.

  - **tools**: Includes the tools used by Genesis to handle some special functions.

  - **widgets**: Contains the theme specific widgets.

As you can see, if you choose to look through Genesis, the directories will help you quickly identify the files you need.

I could write several sections on each directory, but this chapter focuses on integrating the actions with the Framework, which means looking in the structure directory.

The files in the structure directory include almost every action used in Genesis.

How do you know exactly what code removes a given element on the site? You need to know the directory that has the original action. If I don't know the answer off the top of my head, I can quickly find it by searching the right directory.

Let's look at the files in the structure directory.

- **archive.php**: This has the actions specific to archive pages, like the archive title output.

- **comments.php**: This includes actions specific to the comments on the site, like the comment form.

- **footer.php**: This contains the footer actions, including the new widgeted footer.

- **header.php**: Here you'll find the actions that load on hooks in the header.php, including the site title.

- **layout.php**: These are actions that handle loading the sidebars.

- **loops.php**: This handles the three loops available in Genesis: standard, custom, and grid loops.

- **menu.php**: This controls the menu output.

- **post.php**: Essentially this is everything that loads inside the loop.

- **search.php**: This has actions specific to search pages.

- **sidebar.php**: This includes the hooks and actions that create the sidebars, if they are loaded by the layout.php file.

The file structure does make it easy to find the code you're looking for. The names are essentially an index for the functions.

WORKING WITH GENESIS HOOKS

OK, enough of the preliminary details. You came here for specific examples on how to work with the hooks.

In the section below, I'm going to break this down into three parts:

• Removing actions

• Moving actions

• Modifying actions

In each part, I'll give a specific example from the Genesis files with explanations on what is happening. I'll also explain how you can use that information to do this on your own with other actions.

Removing Actions

I'm starting with removing actions, because that is the most straightforward task.

In the chapter "Genesis Actions Explained," we saw that removing an action is a matter of having the exact same action, but with "remove" instead of "add". So this is the process of removing an action:

• Find the action you want to remove.

• Copy it into your child theme's functions.php file.

• Change "add" to "remove".

In this example, we're removing the the "post_info" action. The StudioPress site also has a short guide on doing this: http://ostra.in/post-info.

What do we know about this?

• Well, we know it is in the loop. We know that because it appears on every post in an archive view (one that shows multiple posts on a page).

- OK, now look at the files. Which one says it deals with loop actions? Yes, it's in the post.php file.
- Open the post.php file, and try to see if you can find the right code.

```
add_filter('genesis_post_info', 'do_shortcode',
20);

add_action('genesis_before_post_content',
'genesis_post_info');

/**

* Add the post info (byline) under the title

*

* @since 0.2.3

*/

function genesis_post_info() {

if ( is_page() )

return; // don't do post-info on pages

$post_info = '[post_date] ' . __('By',
'genesis') . ' [post_author_posts_link]
[post_comments] [post_edit]';

printf( '<div class="post-info">%s</div>',
apply_filters('genesis_post_info', $post_info)
);
```

```
}
```

OK, now we have the code needed. Notice there is a "filter," an "action," and a "function".

- The "filter" is for another chapter, so let's ignore that for now.
- We don't need to "function" to remove or move an action, so we can ignore that.
- All we need is line two that starts with "add_action" from this section of code.
- Copy that into the functions.php file of your child theme, and change "add" to "remove".

This is the code we end up with:

```
remove_action('genesis_before_post_content',
'genesis_post_info');
```

Moving Actions

The first part of moving an action is removing the action. Think of it like a cut-and-paste in Microsoft Word. If you want to move some code, first you cut it, then you add it back in where you want it. Another helpful tutorial on the StudioPress site shows how to move the navigation menus: http://ostra.in/move-header.

Let's see if we can use our new knowledge to replicate moving the navigation menu by looking at the code.

- First, we need to know what file to look in.
- Since we are dealing with the menu, the answer should be pretty apparent ... yep, the menu.php file.

- For this we want to move the primary navigation. Nothing too fancy, we just want it above the header instead of below it.

Did you find the code for the primary navigation menu yet? I'm not going to copy it all here, but this is the relevant part:

```
add_action('genesis_after_header',
'genesis_do_nav');

/**

* This function is responsible for displaying
the "Primary Navigation" bar.

*

* @uses genesis_nav(), genesis_get_option(),
wp_nav_menu()

* @since 1.0

*/

function genesis_do_nav() {
```

In order to move the action, you first need to remove it.

- Just copy the action into the child theme functions.php file.
- Change "add" to "remove".

Now you need to move the action somewhere else.

- Paste the code again.
- Then, change the hook.

With some effort you can memorize all the hooks, but there is a handy hook reference in the first chapter to help you out.

- Since we want it to go before the header, we can change it from "genesis_after_header" to "genesis_before_header".

This is the code we end up with:

```
remove_action('genesis_after_header',
'genesis_do_nav');

add_action('genesis_before_header',
'genesis_do_nav');
```

Modifying Actions

This is the hardest thing when dealing with Genesis Actions. You have to remove the existing action, then create your own function to replace it.

One of the most common changes done in child themes is the need for a custom loop. This can be done in several ways, but for the sake of this example, we are going to remove the existing loop and replace it with a custom loop using "genesis_custom_loop()".

Since we are working with loops, which file should we open? If you said loops.php, then you are correct.

- So go ahead and open the loops.php file.
- The code is right at the top of the file.

```
add_action('genesis_loop', 'genesis_do_loop');
```

That was easy. This loads a function that decides which loop to load, and we will be bypassing that. I'm going to skip to the final code, so I can explain what I would add to the child theme, and how this can be done with other actions:

```
remove_action( 'genesis_loop',
'genesis_do_loop' );

add_action(    'genesis_loop', 'child_do_loop'
   );

function child_do_loop() {

global $query_string;

$args = array( 'cat' => -1, 'order' => 'ASC' );

$args = wp_parse_args( $query_string, $args );

genesis_custom_loop( $args );

}
```

OK, if you've been following along, you should know the following.

- The first line just removes the existing loop function.
- The second line adds our custom loop function. It must have a unique name. I often change "genesis" to the name of the child theme. If this were added in an archive.php file, I might go with "child_do_archive_loop" instead.
- Also notice that line three defines the function, and it exactly matches the function name in the action. This is very important as well.

The guts of this is creating the "$args" for the custom loop.

- The first part makes the existing query something that can be used inside the function. Any variable not defined in the function needs to be declared global before you can use it. If I wanted to use the "$post->ID", a very common variable from online tutorials, then I would also need to make "$post" global. You can make more than one variable global by using comma separated variables, as shown below.

```
global $post, $query_string;
```

- Moving on, the next lines defines the "$args" variable I'm going to use for the custom query. These are the same args used in "WP_Query" or "query_posts()".

- Since I want to keep the existing query, I need to merge that with the "$args" I defined. The "wp_parse_args()" function does exactly this.

- With my newly merged "$args", I can now run the "genesis_custom_loop()", which basically takes the args to build a new query and then runs that loop using the exact same hooks that are found in the standard loop.

To change some functions, you might be best to start by copying the existing function, giving it a new name, and editing it to what you need it to be. As I said before, there are other options to modifying a function. In a future chapter, I will be explaining filters, which can let you make big changes without removing, adding, or modifying actions.

Now that you know what actions are, how to use them to add, move, and remove existing content, new content, and plugins, you need one more helpful tip.

ADDING DUPLICATE CONTENT

Whether you are adding a tweet button to the top and bottom of your post, putting some extra markup around several elements, or inserting adsense in more than one place, you need to be able to duplicate your code.

One might do this by creating an extra action/function pair, but that isn't really required. In fact, you can use some conditional code so that very similar code is altered depending on where it is being used. This allows you to have one function that is used in more than one place.

In this first example, I am demonstrating a Google Adsense ad being put at the top and bottom of your post content.

```
add_action( 'genesis_before_entry_content',
'child_content_conditional_adsense', 15);
add_action( 'genesis_after_entry_content',
'child_content_conditional_adsense', 5);
/** inserts an adsense ad above and below the
content */
function child_content_adsense() { ?>

<div class="adsense">
<!--insert adsense code-->
</div><!-- end .adsense -->

<?php }
```

Now this exact same code will load just before and after the .entry-content div.

*Note: This code is using the "entry" hooks. The next example will use the "post" hooks. The difference is the newer HTML5 themes use "entry", where the older XHTML themes use "post".

If I wanted to handle the markup differently, then I need to know which hook I'm loading on. This is handled conditionally, which I will explain in more detail in a bonus chapter. This code handles what we need though.

```
add_action( 'genesis_before_post_content',
'child_content_conditional_adsense', 15);
```

```
add_action( 'genesis_after_post_content',
'child_content_conditional_adsense', 5);
/** inserts an adsense ad above and below the
content with a conditional class. */
function child_content_conditional_adsense() {
?>

<div class="adsense <?php echo
'genesis_before_post_content' ==
current_filter() ? 'before' : 'after'; ?>">
<!--insert adsense code-->
</div><!-- end .adsense -->

<?php }
```

This doesn't look like a traditional conditional statement, but it is a very efficient way of assigning a variable value or echoing a statement like this.

- The first part says it is to echo (that is print that in the code at that location).
- The next part, up to the "?", tells it the condition it is to look for.
- The "?" tells it what string to use if the condition is true, in this case of the current_filter() is "genesis_before_post_content".
- The code after the ":" tells it what to show when it isn't on that hook.

Now it can be styled as "before" and "after" so you can float one block left and the other right, or whatever.

WHAT'S NEXT?

Currently you can find actions in the Genesis files and then remove, move, or modify them. That's a pretty good start.

In the next chapter, we will start looking at filters. These gave me a lot of trouble starting out, but by the time you finish the chapter, you will be way ahead of where I was when I first started working with Genesis.

CHAPTER 6.

GENESIS FILTERS EXPLAINED

In the last two chapters, we talked about actions in Genesis. For the next three chapters we're going to focus on the filters within Genesis.

Like the chapter "Actions Explained," this chapter is intended to explain the actual functions. Since the functions themselves are not significantly different from the action functions, this chapter will be shorter and heavily reference the "Actions Explained" chapter.

WHAT ARE FILTERS?

Filters are functions that change other functions.

I often refer to filters as "voodoo" because they feel like some kind of magic to me, even though I know how they work and use them more and more frequently. In fact, many contributions I've made to the Genesis core development have been to increase the number of available filters, because it really does make it easier to do a lot of big things with less code.

To use the Lego analogy again, if an action says "add this set of blocks to this location," a filter says "before you do that, change this one block." For example, a filter in Lego might say, "use a green block instead of a blue bloc."

With an action you have to provide an instruction to remove the block of code, then another instruction to add a new block of code, plus provide the newly altered code. That is a lot of work when you can say "I just want to change this one thing."

The filter directly changes the color of the block without removing it and putting a different colored block in place.

Of course, I'm sure you can see why this feels like voodoo, or cheating. It's too easy when you think of it like that. Things shouldn't be that easy, so there has to be a catch. Well, there is: you can only use filters to change something that has filters applied to it.

APPLY FILTERS

A mistake a lot of people make is thinking you can filter any function. This happens because the "filter name" often matches the function. Developers do this because we are lazy, and it is much easier to remember it that way.

Someone on the inside can tell if they can use a filter by looking at the function, and now you can too because I'm breaking open the big secret.

- Look for the "apply_filters()" function.

- It should look similar to the function below.

```
apply_filters( $tag, $value, $var1, $var2, ...
);
```

This has a couple of important parts.

- The "$tag" is the filter name. We'll talk about it in more detail later. In fact, we'll talk about all of these in more detail later.

- The "$value" is the value that can be edited or replaced.

- The "$var1", "$var2"… are variables that can be used to get additional information, which is useful for conditional statements. For example, `if ( 'blue' == $var1 ) return 'color';`, or for `str_replace()` searches and plenty of other helpful uses. You can't directly change the $var content though.

In short, if you find this function on a value you want to change, then you can save a lot of time instead of having to work with actions.

There are a ton of filters in WordPress, not just Genesis. In fact, Genesis uses some of the WordPress filters too.

ADDING FILTERS

The actual function "add_filter()" has the exact same five parts as "add_action", which we saw in an earlier chapter. Let's get a quick refresher:

1. **Instruction Type:** This is going to be "add" or "remove".
2. **The Filter to be Used**: That is what you are going to modify.
3. **The Call Back Function**: This is the function that will change the value of the filter.
4. **The Priority**: This shows what order the callback is loaded relative to other actions.
5. **Accepted Args**: This is the number of variables that can be sent to the function.

```
/**
 * Generic function with a filter.
 */
function hook_function() {

    echo esc_html( apply_filters(
'hook_filter', 'foo', 'var 1', 'var 2', 'var 3'
) );
```

```
}

add_filter( 'hook_filter', 'filter_function',
10, 2 );

/**
 * Changes the value of hook_filter if $var1 ==
'var 1'
 *
 * @param string $value The value that will be
filtered.
 * @param string $var1  Argument being checked.
 *
 * @returns string
 */
function filter_function( $value, $var1 ){

    if ( 'var 1' === $var1 ) {
        return 'bar';
    }

    return $value;

}
```

Now let's look at this more closely.

You should already be familiar with the action. It is loading the code onto the "hook". All it does is put "foo" on the screen where that hook is at. Before it can do that though, it applies any filters. In other words, it looks for any changes to the instructions.

The "add_filter" line is adding a filter to that. I have given it a function to run. However, I told it I only want two arguments, so it will get the "$value" and "$var1". If I had told it I want three arguments, it would use the "$value" and the first two $vars. So if I need the third $var, I have to tell it I want four arguments. Even if I don't use the first two $vars in my code, they have to have a value so the one I want will be loaded for me to get that value.

In the guts of this, I have it check to see if the $var matches a specific string, which it will since I'm not writing a dynamic function that might have different values in different scenarios. Then I have it telling it to return "bar". This replaces the $value (foo) with "bar" so that will print instead.

This is a very important distinction. The final value must always be returned, not echoed. I have been frustrated time and time again with developers writing plugins who will filter the_content and echo their edited content instead of returning it. If you don't return the value, then all other filters have nothing to work with. That is bad programming, and just plain rude. Always return the "$value".

By the way, the last line also returns the "$value". This is so that the unedited value gets returned. A better way to write this is:

```
add_filter( 'hook_filter', 'filter_function',
10, 2 );

/**
 * Changes the value of hook_filter if $var1 ==
'var 1'
 *
 * @param string $value The value that will be
filtered.
 * @param string $var1  Argument being checked.
 *
 * @returns string
 */
function filter_function( $value, $var1 ){
```

```
if ( 'var 1' === $var1 ) {
    $value = 'bar';
}


return $value;


}
```

This is better because the "$value" is returned by default. When the condition matches, the value is altered. It means there is one return statement and less chance to mess it up.

In more complex filters, it may be necessary to have multiple returns, so a third pattern to consider is having a condition at the top to check if the filter should be edited. If it doesn't, you should return the unedited value right away. This will prevent accidentally editing it later and simplifying the code.

REMOVING FILTERS

The "remove_filter()" function is identical in use to the "remove_action()" function. It needs to match the "add_filter()" exactly and has to come after the filter was added.

```
add_filter( 'hook_filter', 'filter_function',
10, 2 );
remove_filter( 'hook_filter',
'filter_function', 10, 2 );
```

WHAT'S NEXT?

If you feel a bit like you've just read some ancient mystical tome, it's OK- I feel like I just wrote one. The next chapter will use some specific examples from Genesis to show how to make changes without using actions.

Just for fun, I'll also show how to make the change with actions first, in order to demonstrate how much more efficient filters are.

CHAPTER 7.

GENESIS FRAMEWORK FILTERS EXPLAINED

In the previous chapter, I went over the basics of how the add/ remove filter function works.

We saw that filters work more efficiently than actions when changing existing content rather than adding new content. The trick is finding where filters exist.

In "Genesis Framework Actions Explained," I showed where to find most of the actions used in Genesis. Many of the filters you will need can be found in the same files. A few notable exceptions exist. There are several filters available in the genesis/ lib/classes/breadcrumb.php file and in the files within genesis/ lib/functions/ folder. The names of the files should help identify the contents of the folders. I'll be addressing those files later in the book when we talk about Genesis functions.

WHAT IS A STRING?

Before we dive into this chapter, let's review the concept of a "string".

In PHP, there are a few different kinds of data. These are strings, arrays, objects, integers, and floats. Technically this might be an over-simplification, but for the sake of what we are covering, that is enough.

The simplest definition is that a string is text. This can include HTML, because HTML is really just text.

REPLACING A STRING

Now that we have some basic idea of what a string is, lets look for one to replace. If someone does a search and no posts are returned, it will say "Sorry, no posts matched your criteria." That's fine, but what if I want to say that message to say something else?

This message is run inside the loop, which means we should start by looking in the post.php file. The file called loop.php builds the loop structure, but post.php creates the actual output within the loop. Inside that file we will find:

```
add_action('genesis_loop_else',
'genesis_do_noposts');
/**
* No Posts
*/
function genesis_do_noposts() {

printf( '<p>%s</p>', apply_filters(
'genesis_noposts_text', __('Sorry, no posts
matched your criteria.', 'genesis') ) );

}
```

Thinking back to the previous chapter on filters, you will remember that the "apply_filters()" function is the place where the magic happens. It looks like a lot is going on, but really there is just one string there: the "__()" function is used for localizing the text.

If you don't need to translate your theme, then you can skip it and just put your string in directly. In this example, we'll leave it in as a best practice. Remember, you will have to update your localization files if you make changes to the string the files are looking for.

Lt's check the code and go through how it works.

```
add_filter( 'genesis_noposts_text',
'child_noposts_text' );
/**
 * Changes the No Posts text for search pages.
 *
 * @param string $text The no posts text.
 *
 * @returns string
 */
function child_noposts_text( $text ) {
    if( ! is_search() ) {
        return $text;
    }

    return '<span class="no-posts">' .
esc_html__( 'Sorry, no posts were found for
your search.', 'child' ) . '</span>';
}
```

You should notice three things.

1. The priority and number of accepted arguments aren't specified. We are using the default of "10, 1", so it doesn't have to be added.
2. We are returning the "$text" if it isn't the search page. This is the third pattern I mentioned, but didn't provide an example of, in the previous chapter. We do this early on so we don't forget later, but it could be done at the end as well.
3. We return the internationalized string that should appear on search pages without a valid response. I'm building an

HTML string with some PHP, so I have to put them together with ".".

Alternatively, you can skip this last step if you aren't using an internationalized string. If that's the case, just put:

```
return '<span class="no-posts">Sorry, no posts
were found for your search.</span>';
```

You also don't need this if you aren't adding the extra HTML. I personally like to be able to target the results, so I put the HTML in with the internationalized string.

CHANGING STRINGS

Changing strings is slightly different from replacing strings. When changing strings, you will be retaining some portion of the existing string and building something new, either by adding on, or using some advanced techniques like "str_replace()" or "preg_replace()".

One of the more common tasks people want to do is change the footer. There is a handy plugin to do that called "Genesis Simple Edits," but if you are building a child theme or need to use PHP, that plugin won't work.

So let's see if that might be filterable.

- We know from the "Genesis Framework Actions Explained" chapter that the footer actions are in genesis/lib/structure/footer.php.

- Check there to see if the filters are in that same file.

- At the end of the "genesis_do_footer()" function, you will find this line of code:

```
echo apply_filters( 'genesis_footer_output',
$output, $backtotop_text, $creds_text );
```

- We also know that the "$output" can be changed or replaced, and we can also make use of the "$backtotop_text" and "$creds_text". These are args with values that can be edited or used with the "str_replace()" function, which is what we'll do here.

```
add_filter( 'genesis_footer_output',
'child_footer_output', 10, 3);
/**
 * Modifies the footer text.
 *
 * @param string $output         The footer
output.
 * @param string $backtotop_text The back to
top portion of the footer.
 * @param string $creds_text     The credits
portion of the footer.
 *
 * @returns string
 */
function child_footer_output( $output,
$backtotop_text, $creds_text ) {

    $child_creds_text = 'Copyright 2007 - '.
date( 'Y' ) .'<a
href="http://designsbynickthegeek.com">Nick the
Geek</a>';

    $output = str_replace( $creds_text,
$child_creds_text, $output );

    return $output;
}
```

This is making things a little complex for what I've done here. I could have just done a simple replace on the "genesis_footer_creds_text" filter hook, but then I couldn't show one way of using "str_replace()" to change the string value. There are times when this is the best solution, so it is important to see how this works.

Line 5 sets up the text we will be adding.

Line 6 includes a string with a start date for the copyright and the current year as the end date. I've found a lot of people want to know how to do this, so now you know how.

All the other stuff in the footer went away. Remember, any html including plain text can go inside the single quotes (apostrophes), but the php has to go outside. To build the string, you put the "." between string values. There is another really cool way to do this using a function that I'll explain later.

I skipped the get text functions that would internationalize (make it possible to translate/localize) the content. I did this because I'm assuming this is for my site, and it will never need to be localized. There are times where you don't need to provide a way to localize content, but if there is a chance it might ever be put in another language or even regional localization, you should take the time to do it right.

Line 7 uses "str_replace()" to find the "$creds_text" inside the "$output" and replace it with the "$new_creds_text".

I'm sure you can see how this simple function can come in very handy when you have a string you want to modify, but it has already been joined together in the string that can be filtered.

WHAT'S NEXT?

I'm sure you can see why I refer to filters as a kind of voodoo. They can be difficult to grasp when starting out, and many developers will want to fall back to actions to accomplish the same end. However, with some practice filters will become your preferred method. In fact, you will start pestering the folks behind Genesis and WordPress to include more filters to save you time and code.

In the next chapter, we'll work on some more techniques in the next chapter. We'll specifically focusing on working with arrays, which are a kind of complex string.

CHAPTER 8.

GENESIS FILTERS WITH ARRAYS EXPLAINED

In the previous two chapters, we've seen how filters work in Genesis.

The last chapter dealt with using filters to change "strings", or simple text and HTML phrases. I demonstrated simple replacement as well as a more advanced technique for changing a string within the string.

This chapter will use similar examples and techniques, but will focus on objects, or arrays.

WHAT IS AN ARRAY?

You can think of an array as an ordered group of strings.

There are two parts to an array, the key and the value.

They can be assigned in a few different ways and will show up in the code differently based on how the value is being assigned. Here is a simple example:

```
$array_1      = array(
    'key1' => 'value1',
    'key2' => 'value2',
);
$array_2       = array( 'value1', 'value2' );
```

```
$array_2[]    = 'value3';
$array_2['3'] = 'value4';
```

- In the "array_1" example, the keys are listed as "key1" with a string value of "value1" and "key2" with a string value of "value2".

- In the "array_2" example, the keys aren't listed. So, they are automatically assigned as 0 and 1.

- The next example would have a key of 2, and it is put onto the end of the existing "$array_2" string.

- The last "$array_2['3']" example manually assigns the key of "3" the value of "value4".

One interesting thing to note here is key "2" with the value of "value3" is an integer, while key "3" with the value of "value4" is a string. This doesn't matter most of the time, but it is important in certain circumstances, so keep that in the back of your head.

An interesting thing about arrays in PHP is that they can contain different kinds of data. It is possible for an array to have just strings like the examples above, but they can also have numbers, objects or even other arrays like this:

```
$array_1 = array(
    'odd'  => array( 1, 3, 5 ),
    'even' => array( 2, 4, 6 ),
);
```

In this case "$array_1" is made of two object arrays, one with odd numbers and the other with even numbers.

The reason arrays are built is because they are efficient ways of storing related information without needing to have dozens, hundreds, or even thousands of separate variables. The information can then be unpacked using a variety of different methods.

ADDING TO AN ARRAY

This might be the simplest way of working with an array, but it is also tricky because you need to know what values will be useful. A great example would be working with the comment form. Genesis uses this code to create the comment form:

```
add_action( 'genesis_comment_form',
'genesis_do_comment_form' );
/**
 * Optionally show the comment form.
 *
 * Genesis asks WP for the HTML5 version of the
comment form - it uses {@link
genesis_comment_form_args()} to revert to
 * XHTML form fields when child theme does not
support HTML5.
 *
 * @since 1.0.0
 *
 * @return void Return early if comments are
closed via Genesis for this page or post.
 */
function genesis_do_comment_form() {

    // Bail if comments are closed for this post
type.
    if ( ( is_page() && ! genesis_get_option(
'comments_pages' ) ) || ( is_single() && !
genesis_get_option( 'comments_posts' ) ) ) {
        return;
    }
```

```
    comment_form( array(
        'format' => 'html5',
    ) );


}


add_filter( 'comment_form_defaults',
'genesis_comment_form_args' );
/**
 * Filter the default comment form arguments,
used by `comment_form()`.
 *
 * Applies only to XHTML child themes, since
Genesis uses default HTML5 comment form where
possible.
 *
 * Applies `genesis_comment_form_args` filter.
 *
 * @since 1.8.0
 *
 * @global string $user_identity Display name
of the user.
 *
 * @param array $defaults Comment form default
arguments.
 * @return array Filtered comment form default
arguments.
 */
function genesis_comment_form_args( array
$defaults ) {

    // Use WordPress default HTML5 comment form
if themes supports HTML5.
    if ( genesis_html5() ) {
        return $defaults;
```

```php
	}

	global $user_identity;

	$commenter = wp_get_current_commenter();
	$req       = get_option(
'require_name_email' );
	$aria_req  = ( $req ? '
aria-required="true"' : '' );

	$author = '<p class="comment-form-author">' .
			'<input id="author" name="author"
type="text" value="' . esc_attr(
$commenter['comment_author'] ) . '" size="30"
tabindex="1"' . $aria_req . ' />' .
			'<label for="author">' . __(
'Name', 'genesis' ) . '</label> ' .
			( $req ? '<span
class="required">*</span>' : '' ) .
			'</p>';

	$email = '<p class="comment-form-email">' .
			'<input id="email" name="email"
type="text" value="' . esc_attr(
$commenter['comment_author_email'] ) . '"
size="30" tabindex="2"' . $aria_req . ' />' .
			'<label for="email">' . __(
'Email', 'genesis' ) . '</label> ' .
			( $req ? '<span
class="required">*</span>' : '' ) .
			'</p>';

	$url = '<p class="comment-form-url">' .
			'<input id="url" name="url"
type="text" value="' . esc_attr(
```

```
$commenter['comment_author_url'] ) . '"
size="30" tabindex="3" />' .
        '<label for="url">' . __( 'Website',
'genesis' ) . '</label>' .
        '</p>';

    $comment_field = '<p
class="comment-form-comment">' .
                    '<textarea id="comment"
name="comment" cols="45" rows="8" tabindex="4"
aria-required="true"></textarea>' .
                    '</p>';

    $args = array(
        'comment_field'         => $comment_field,
        'title_reply'           => __( 'Speak Your
Mind', 'genesis' ),
        'comment_notes_before' => '',
        'comment_notes_after'  => '',
        'fields'                => array(
            'author' => $author,
            'email'  => $email,
            'url'    => $url,
        ),
    );

    // Merge $args with $defaults.
    $args = wp_parse_args( $args, $defaults );

    // Return filterable array of $args, along
with other optional variables.
    return apply_filters(
'genesis_comment_form_args', $args,
$user_identity, get_the_ID(), $commenter, $req,
$aria_req );
```

}

OK, now let's get ready for some advanced filtering.

Once upon a time, this was done with the arguments going directly to the "comment_form()" function. Now you can use a very simple "comment_form" with a complex filter being applied to those arguments.

There are quite a few arguments being passed via that filter, so it looks big and scary, but we aren't going to need to deal with all of it.

For the purpose of this book, we will be changing the submit button text, which means we need to add to the list of arguments.

Now we can unhook the action and add a new action with our own function that has this full list, plus the "label_submit" value (see the codex article).

However, that would be a lot of unneeded code. In comparison, let's see how simple this is with a filter.

```
add_filter( 'genesis_comment_form_args',
'child_comment_form_args' );
/**
 * Changes the Submit Comment button copy.
 *
 * @param array $args The Genesis comment form
arguments.
 *
 * @return array
 */
function child_comment_form_args( $args ) {
    $args['label_submit'] = __( 'Publish
Comment', 'child' );
```

```
    return $args;
}
```

That's all it takes. Now let's look at it to see what happens.

- The first line adds the filter. It could include up to six arguments in the function, but we only need the one. So in this case, the default is fine.
- The second line defines our function.
- The next line adds the "label_submit" key to the "$args" array with a value of "Publish Comment". We know this value matters because we looked at the WordPress codex article and saw it is a valid argument for the function.
- All that is left is to return the object to be used in the "comment_form()" function.

REPLACING ARRAY VALUES

Replacing a value is much easier, since you can look in the file and replace the currently assigned value. There is no need to figure out what hidden values might work.

One place you might do this is with the breadcrumbs arguments. Let's look at the file. This one is a bit trickier to find. It isn't in the genesis/lib/structure/ files, nor the genesis/lib/functions/ files. The last likely place, since it isn't an admin function, is in genesis/lib/classes/. Fortunately, there is a breadcrumb.php file in that folder.

Now this is a class, and reading it is a tiny bit different. Let me help by posting the code we will be working with. Then I will explain how to know what is happening.

```
/**
 * Constructor. Set up cacheable values and
```

```
settings.
 *
 * @since 1.5
 *
 * @param array $args
 */
function genesis_breadcrumb() {
$this->on_front = get_option( 'show_on_front' );

/** Default arguments **/
$this->args = array(
 'home'                        => __( 'Home',
'genesis' ),
 'sep'                         => ' / ',
 'list_sep'                    => ', ',
 'prefix'                      => '<div
class="breadcrumb">',
 'suffix'                      => '</div>',
 'heirarchial_attachments'     => true,
 'heirarchial_categories'      => true,
 'display'                     => true,
 'labels'                      => array(
 'prefix'                      => __( 'You are
here: ', 'genesis' ),
 'author'                      => __( 'Archives for
', 'genesis' ),
 'category'                    => __( 'Archives for
', 'genesis' ),
 'tag'                         => __( 'Archives for
', 'genesis' ),
 'date'                        => __( 'Archives for
', 'genesis' ),
 'search'                      => __( 'Search for
', 'genesis' ),
 'tax'                         => __( 'Archives for
```

```
', 'genesis' ),
 'post_type'                    => __( 'Archives for
', 'genesis' ),
 '404'                          => __( 'Not found:
', 'genesis' )
)
);

}

/**
 * Return the final completed breadcrumb in
markup wrapper. Public.
 *
 * @since 1.5
 *
 * @return string HTML markup
 */
function get_output( $args = array() ) {
    /** Merge and Filter user and default
arguments **/
    $this->args = apply_filters(
'genesis_breadcrumb_args', wp_parse_args(
$args, $this->args ) );

    return $this->args['prefix'] .
$this->args['labels']['prefix'] .
$this->build_crumbs() . $this->args['suffix'];
}
```

That's a lot of code, and there is a lot more in the file, but this is what is relevant.

The most important line would be line 46, I highlighted it so you don't miss it. I highlighted a couple other lines because those are the ones we will be changing.

Line 46 is special because it includes "apply_filters()", which means we can change the value of something. The something is the `get_output( $args )` and `$this->args`.

If you look up to line 12, you will see `$this->args`, which is what we want to change.

Perfect. Ok, so now lets change those values.

```
add_filter( 'genesis_breadcrumb_args',
'child_breadcrumb_args' );
/**
 * Changes the breadcrumb arguments.
 *
 * @param array $args The breadcrumb args.
 *
 * @returns array
 */
function child_breadcrumb_args( $args ) {
    $args['sep']                  = ' | ';
    $args['labels']['prefix']   = __( 'Path to
here: ', 'child' );
    $args['labels']['category'] = __(
'Category: ', 'child' );

    return $args;
}
```

- As you can see, all we have to do is provide the same key, and then we can change the value.
- In the case of nested values like the "labels" object, you need to provide the key of the object (labels), then the string (prefix and category).
- Finally, always remember to return your array when you are done with it.

CHANGING AN ARRAY

If you've been following along, you should have an idea of what to expect here. Basically we are going to use a string replace to change part of a value.

For this example we will be removing some invalid markup. The specific markup can be left, and generally I'd recommend leaving it alone. Sometimes you have very strict validation requirements, so you have to remove certain HTML that is used for accessibility to achieve those requirements.

In this case I am referring to the aria-require attribute in the comment form. We have to go back to the genesis/lib/structure/comments.php file for this one.

We could replace any value with the aria-required attribute, but that is quite a bit of code. Changing part of the value is much more efficient.

```php
add_filter( 'genesis_comment_form_args',
'child_comment_form_remove_aria_required' );
/**
 * Remove aria in comments on XHTML themes.
 *
 * @param array $args The comment form args.
 *
 * @returns array
 */
function
child_comment_form_remove_aria_required( $args
){
    $args          = str_replace( '
aria-required="true"', '', $args );
    $args[fields] = str_replace( '
aria-required="true"', '', $args[fields] );
```

```
    return $args;
}
```

The first two lines should look very familiar. The important thing to note is that I used a different callback function from the first example. If I had two functions with the same name, the site would break. Always give your functions unique names. The first two lines in the function are changing the values.

- Any string in the "$args" array that had ' aria-required="true"' won't after the first.

- Any of the strings in the "fields" object will have lost the attribute after the second.

- Once again, always remember to return your value when done.

WHAT'S NEXT?

This concludes the filters section. I hope the haze is starting to lift. Filters may still feel like some kind of dark magic you want to learn, but are a bit afraid of. I can totally relate to that feeling. Because the subject can be hazy at best when you first start down this path, I don't want to overwhelm you right now, but I'm including some tutorials in the bonus section that make use of filters.

Remember, filters are constructed just like actions, and you can use them to change values, not just add content like with actions.

Now that you have an idea of where to find filters and how to use them to work with arrays, we will be moving on to functions. The next chapter will explain functions and give a brief overview of the organization of functions in Genesis.

CHAPTER 9.

GENESIS FUNCTIONS EXPLAINED

So far we've talked about actions and filters, but Genesis is so much more than that. One of the great things about Genesis is all the helper functions.

In this chapter, I am going to give you an overview of functions in Genesis.

You'll see how to find the Genesis functions and how to understand those functions. You'll also get an overview of the Genesis helper functions, a quick look at the top Genesis functions, and as a bonus I'll show how to make your own functions.

WHAT IS A FUNCTION?

When someone is getting started with development, they often spend all of their energy copying code and don't learn what that code is doing.

This approach works until you add a security vulnerability to your site or take the entire site down. Even more importantly, this scattered approach will limit your ability to modify the code to best suit your needs.

So let's take a moment to discover what a function is.

A function is a block of repeatable code.

That is really the long and short of it. Any time you write the same code more than once, you can turn that into a function. However, it becomes more complex as you begin to do similar things. For example, lets say you have some code that outputs some HTML like this:

```
<div class="highlight">Some text</div>.
```

Only you need to change the part that says "some text" when it shows up. You can just keep typing `<div class="highlight">Some other text</div>` or you can make a function that does this for you, which will save you time and make your code smaller and more efficient.

At the end of this chapter I'll show you how to do that, but first let's look at the six parts of a function.

THE SIX PARTS OF A FUNCTION

Writing a function sounds like a monumental task, especially to people who are new to PHP. The good news is that it is really pretty easy. The function breaks down into a few key parts. Lets looks at a generic function:

```
function generic( $arg='foo' ) {

    echo $arg;

}
```

This is as simple as it gets. There are six parts to a basic function. Let's look at them in more detail:

1. The Word "function"

The word "function" tells PHP this is a function that must be remembered so you can use it later.

2. The Function Name

The next part, "generic", is the function name. This is how you call for the code to be executed.

Let's talk function names for a second. "generic" is a terrible name for a function. It is too short, non-descriptive, and … well generic. The length itself isn't a problem. PHP doesn't require a minimum number of characters. The shortness is only a problem because it prevents it from being unique and descriptive.

A function name must be unique. You can't have two functions with the same name. If you do, then you will get an error that will break your site.

This is why the code in the StudioPress site and support forums will include functions like "child_do_title". It is unlikely that a plugin author is using the child prefix. I personally use the "ntg" prefix (short for "Nick the Geek") on my custom code, so I will know right away that I wrote the code for that. A child theme will typically use the child theme name or abbreviation, this makes it less likely to cause a problem with two functions having the same name.

A function name should also be descriptive. This isn't mandatory. I could have a function called "child_function_a" that handles the title output, and so long as I don't have another function with that name, it will work. However, I'm unlikely to remember that name when I need it and will probably forget what it does. "child_do_title" is much better because it tells me that it is a function in my child theme, and it "does the title" or outputs the title. If I write a function documentation block, then

I'll know all I need to know a year from now when I'm looking at my theme.

3. The Argument

The next part of the function "($arg = 'foo')" is the "argument" for the function. Functions don't require the argument, and a function can have multiple arguments.

In this case I am providing a "default" value for my argument, but it can be overridden when the function is called.

If I don't have an argument, it will be written like "function generic(){}", and most of the time that is what you will do.

On a side note, this function only "echos" the argument. That means it puts that value in where the function is. So, if I run that function, it will be replaced with "foo", unless I write it into my code like "generic('bar');". Then, my defined "$arg" is replaced, and it will put "bar" on the screen instead of "foo." This will make more sense when we go into more depth on using the function in the hook.

4. The Curly Brace {

After the argument is the curly brace, "{", to start the function.

5. The Guts of the Function

Everything after the curly brace "{" is the "guts" of the function. It is the code that will be run when the function is invoked (more on this later). The "guts" here would be the "echo $args;" line.

6. The Closing Curly Brace }

The closing curly brace, "}", that ends this section of code signals the PHP engine to stop.

USING HTML IN FUNCTIONS

A function can store HTML code, if needed:

```
function generic_html() {
?>

    Now I'm in HTML, this will print out using
whatever <strong>HTML</strong> markup I give it.

<?php
}
```

You can even merge HTML and PHP like you might when editing a template file with another theme:

```
function generic_html_php() {
?>

    <p>See, still in HTML, no need for any
fancy PHP, unless I need something dynamic,
like the date <?php echo date(); ?>.</p>

    <p>Pretty easy, and that date function
loads inline just like it would in a template
file</p>

<?php
}
```

LOOKING INSIDE THE FILES

Let's look at the files that run Genesis functions. Just like everything else in Genesis, the folders and file names will help us quickly find what we are after.

Let's begin with reviewing what's inside the genesis/lib/functions/ folder.

- **breadcrumb.php**: Includes two functions that create breadcrumb output.
- **compat.php**: Adds PHP compatibility functions for when the server doesn't have them activated.
- **deprecated.php**: Includes functions that shouldn't be used any longer since they have been replaced by new functions.
- **feed.php**: Action and filter, with their functions to redirect the feed.
- **formatting.php**: Includes functions to format text or returned values of other functions.
- **general.php**: Includes functions that don't fit in well with others. Often these will build until a logical group can be formed and a new file is added.
- **head.php**: Includes mostly the SEO functions but also the favicon function.
- **image.php**: Includes functions for retrieving the thumbnails.
- **layout.php**: Includes functions to change the layout/layout options of the site.
- **markup.php**: Includes functions used to create HTML5 aware output. Very helpful for theme developers.
- **menu.php**: Includes the genesis_nav() function.
- **options.php**: Includes functions for retrieving options and custom fields.
- **seo.php**: Includes functions related to theme SEO.
- **upgrade.php**: Handles the theme upgrade.
- **widgetize.php**: Handles creation of default sidebars, footer sidebars, and provides the genesis_register_sidebar() helper function.

THE MOST COMMONLY USED FUNCTIONS

Now that you have some idea of what is in the files, take some time to read through them. I'll be covering most of these files in detail in the following chapters. For now let's look at three of the most often used functions.

genesis_get_image()

This function and genesis_image() work to retrieve the featured image.

Actually it does so much more. It will also pull the first attached image if you forget to set a featured image.

There are several arguments that can be passed, which will will discuss in detail later.

The difference in genesis_get_image() and genesis_image() is that genesis_image() will echo the value returned by genesis_get_image(). This means you don't have to type out "echo" when working with the function. There are plenty of neat tricks you can do as a result of how this works.

genesis_get_custom_field()

Like genesis_get_image(), there is a genesis_custom_field() function that echos the genesis_get_custom_field() value. This uses the $post->ID automatically and only requires the field key.

get_the_content_limit()

Another handy function that can be used as the_content_limit() to directly echo the value. This function uses get_the_content() to retrieve the content and then limit it. This is similar to the_excerpt() but with several advanced featured like easily adjusting the length, more accuracy (character count v word count), and built in read more link.

I know this is just whetting your appetite, but don't worry, soon and very soon I'll be digging into these key functions, all the arguments they take, and any filters you can access to adjust the output.

HOW TO CREATE A FUNCTION

Don't worry, I didn't forget about the promise to use this information to build your own functions.

Let's make a simple function to output that div with the highlight class and the content that is passed to it.

```
/**
 * Outputs HTML that will highlight the text
provided.
 *
 * @param string $text The text that will be
highlighted.
 */
function my_highlighter( $text = '' ) {
    printf( '<div class="highlight">%s</div>',
esc_html( $text ) );
}
```

OK, so do you remember the six parts of the function?

1. **function**: This is the declaration that the following code is a function.
2. **my_highlighter**: This is the function name. It is how you will use this function elsewhere in your code.
3. **($text = ")**: The function arguments. In this case the function takes 1 parameter. Whatever you add to this is output inside the HTML.
4. **{**: The opening curly brace indicates the beginning of the repeatable code.
5. **printf('<div class="highlight">%s</div>', esc_html($text**

));: The function code, aka "guts" of the function. This is run anytime the function is called.

6. }: The closing curly brace. This is the end of the repeatable code. Don't forget this or your code will break.

Now you can build your own functions, but the last bit is hooking those functions into Genesis.

USING YOUR OWN ACTIONS

So you can write a simple function now, but you need to add it to Genesis, right? Well, that's the easy part.

Just write the instructions on what to do with your function. Do you need to have the code executed before the header?

```
add_action( 'genesis_before_header', 'generic'
);
```

You can edit this using the techniques you've learned in the previous sections to adjust the position anywhere relative to the other hooks/actions.

So, now you have a basic idea of how to add your own code to Genesis via hooks, but there is still a good deal to learn.

WORKING WITH EXISTING FUNCTIONS

A common task is integrating a plugin with Genesis. Typically a plugin will include directions like "open your template file and add this code where you want it to appear." This is a daunting task because the files aren't in the child theme, and in Genesis it only has a single line "genesis();".

So how is this done? You need to use actions, like everything else. Depending on what you are doing, this can be extremely easy.

Let's look at the Add to Any plugin. This is generally pretty easy to integrate and should work automatically, but let's say you want to control where the code goes relative to the post meta.

The instructions say to add some code to your template files via the editor.

```php
<?php if( function_exists(
'ADDTOANY_SHARE_SAVE_KIT' ) ) {
ADDTOANY_SHARE_SAVE_KIT(); } ?>
```

You can't do that with Genesis directly, so you need to add it as an action. This can be done like this:

```php
add_action( 'genesis_after_post_content',
'child_do_add_to_any' );

/**
 * add the add to any function after post
content if the function exists
 */
function child_do_add_to_any() {

    if( function_exists(
'ADDTOANY_SHARE_SAVE_KIT' ) ) {
        ADDTOANY_SHARE_SAVE_KIT();
    }


}
```

That's easy enough, but we can streamline this by combining the function and action. Remember, the "callback function" part of the action instruction just says what code to use. Any function will work so long as the function exists, so you can do this instead:

```php
if( function_exists( 'ADDTOANY_SHARE_SAVE_KIT'
```

```
) ) {
    add_action( 'genesis_after_post_content',
'ADDTOANY_SHARE_SAVE_KIT' );
}
```

INVOKING GENESIS FUNCTIONS WITHOUT HOOKS

Invoking a function is fancy-speak for telling a function to run. If you have edited templates in the past, you are probably used to invoking functions without knowing it.

If you add "?php the_content(); ?" or something similar to a file, then you are invoking that function. When you use a hook, you are also invoking a function. You are telling it to load in a specific part of the site before it runs. This means the hooked functions are interchangeable with "normal" functions. Just like you can use another function in a hook, you can use Genesis functions outside the hook.

A great way to do this is in a custom home.php file. You might be editing a child theme with a custom home.php file, but you want a "normal" blog to display after the widgeted content.

- If you look in the genesis/lib/structure/loops.php file you will find that "genesis_do_loop()" invokes "genesis_standard_loop()", so you can just add this in your home.php file where you want the posts to display:

```
<?php genesis_standard_loop(); ?>
```

- This works for any Genesis function. If you want to put the nav menu on the home page. even though it isn't being used elsewhere, you could add it like this:

```
<?php genesis_do_nav(); ?>
```

WHAT'S NEXT?

Now you should have a good grasp of what functions are, how to find various functions in Genesis, and even how to make your own functions.

In the next chapter, we'll look at the General and Formatting functions found inside Genesis.

CHAPTER 10.

GENESIS FORMATTING AND GENERAL FUNCTIONS EXPLAINED

Genesis has dozens of functions, and no-one can remember them all.

Even after working with Genesis for year, I don't bother trying to learn them all. I try to remember the ones I use most often, and then I practice finding other functions.

In this chapter, we will be looking at two of the files in the genesis/lib/functions/ directory:

- formatting.php
- general.php

If you go through the code in those files and read the descriptions here, it will help you to get a feel for where functions can be found. Combined with the details about how functions work from the previous chapter, you will be able to understand the functions you come across in the future.

THE FORMATTING FUNCTIONS

Let's begin by reviewing the Formatting functions, which are located in the formatting.php file. This file focuses on text formatting.

Not all of the functions are likely to be used, but I am going to dig into several of them.

Here is a list of all the functions in the file:

- genesis_truncate_phrase()
- get_the_content_limit()
- genesis_a11y_more_link()
- the_content_limit()
- genesis_rel_nofollow()
- genesis_strip_attr()
- genesis_paged_post_url()
- genesis_sanitize_html_classes()
- genesis_formating_allowedtags()
- genesis_formating_kses()
- genesis_human_time_diff()
- genesis_code()
- genesis_strip_p_tags()

So what do these do and how can you use them?

genesis_truncate_phrase($phrase, $max_characters)

This function is essentially a helper function used by "genesis_get_content_limit()". It has two arguments that are required.

- $phrase is the text to be limited.
- $max_characters is the maximum characters allowed in the text.

You might consider using this anytime you want to limit the text.

For example, I have used it for a custom menu I built for a client that puts a thumbnail with the title in a drop down under a custom taxonomy. Since the titles can get really long, I had to trim them up if they got too long (really who need a 100+ character title?).

Here is some code that does that:

```
echo genesis_truncate_phrase( get_the_title(),
100 );
```

get_the_content_limit($max_char, $more_link_text = '(more...)', $stripteaser = 0)

This is the function that returns the content after trimming it.

The other function, "the_content_limit()", is identical except it automatically echos the value while saving a bit of code.

Both functions take up to three arguments. The second two are optional, they have default values if nothing is passed along.

- The first, "$max_char", is required. It sets the max number of characters allowed in the content before it is trimmed.

- The second,"$more_link_text", is the link anchor text for the "more link". The default is "(more...)".

- The "$stripteaser" content is before the more text, so a ... that isn't linked might be added there. It's default is "0", which is a "null" value, nothing will be output.

The function retrieves the content with "get_the_content()" then strips the tags. This is important, even if it is frustrating, because it prevents errors and provides an accurate count. The errors are open tags.

For example, if you have a link in the middle of where the text is cut off, then you may have an open anchor tag. The same is true for other html elements. After the content is stripped and otherwise prepared, it is trimmed using "genesis_truncate_phrase". Then the more link is built, if available.

This is where the first filter comes up. "get_the_content_more_link" will let you change this link.

The next filter just before the content limit is returned, and "get_the_content_limit" lets you alter the final output. You could use this to wrap it in a div, inject code before, after or even in the middle, or move the $link to the beginning.

"the_content_limit" gives you one more shot at filtering the output with "the_content_limit". However, you won't be able to access the $content, $link, or $max_char variables on that filter.

Here is how you might use it:

```
printf( '<div class="post-teaser">%s</div>',
get_the_content_limit( 300, '[Keep Reading]' )
);
```

This would put the post content, stripped to no more than 300 words, within the post-teaser div.

genesis_a11y_more_link($more_link_text)

This is the first time we've seen "a11y." There is a similar kind of abbreviation "i18n". Both of them work the same way.

It is the first and last letter of the word they stand for and the number of characters in the word.

- "i18n" is "internationalization".
- "a11y" is accessibility.

It is interesting that it ends up looking like "ally", and I think it is important to consider that we are allies with each other, including those who benefit most from accessibility support.

This function has the simple task of adding a bit of content after the "$more_link_text". Before doing so, it checks to see if screen-reader-text is supported using the "genesis_a11y()" function.

genesis_rel_nofollow($xhtml)

This is a simple function to create no follow links.

genesis_strip_attr($xhtml, $elements, $attributes, $two_passes = true)

This function is a pretty complex function, it takes any "$xhtml" text and then uses the provided patterns to remove attributes from specific elements. The "$elements" and "$attributes" can be passed as an array or string.

For an example, look at the "genesis_rel_nofollow()" function. This is used to remove any "rel" attributes from the anchor tags before the "wp_rel_nofollow()" function is used. This prevents the rel value from being added twice, if it happens to be in the value being edited already. This same function might be used to strip titles like:

```
$link = '<a href="http://example.com"
title="title">Anchor Text</a>';
echo genesis_strip_attr( $link, array( 'a' ),
array( 'title' ) );
// outputs "<a href="http://example.com">Anchor
Text</a>"
```

genesis_paged_post_url($i, $post_id = 0)

This function gets the post URL with the paged parameter. This is helpful when a post has paged content and you are building custom navigation directly to the pages.

genesis_sanitize_html_classes($classes, $return_format = 'input')

This function is essentially a wrapper function for the "sanitize_html_class" function. This function ensures that values used to create an HTML class are in the correct format. The "sanitize_html_class" function only accepts strings, but this function will work with an array. So, it is helpful when dealing with an array that will be converted to HTML classes and should be correctly formatted.

genesis_formatting_allowedtags()

This function returns the allowed tags for stripped items. It has a filter that lets you change the values to allow more tags or remove those tags. This is very helpful when using "wp_kses" to allow some HTML in content instead of using the "esc_html" function to ensure the HTML is converted to a safe format. The next function uses wp_kses with this function, so more information can be found there.

genesis_formatting_kses($string)

The "wp_kses()" function is a powerful tool that will remove unsafe HTML but keep HTML that is deemed safe.

Recently I set up a text field to allow end users to add hidden input fields into a form. This is potentially dangerous if other HTML is added because of malicious exploits, but also because adding the wrong kind of HTML in that section would break the layout.

The "wp_kses" function lets me limit the output so only input fields could be added and no other HTML.

This function is a wrapper similar to the "wp_kses_post()" function. It automatically applies "wp_kses" with the arguments from "genesis_formatting_allowedtags()" array.

genesis_human_time_diff($older_date, $newer_date = false, $relative_depth = 2)

This is a super cool function that takes something very tricky and makes it very easy. Basically you pass any two time stamps, and it tells you a human readable difference. If the difference is one hour ago, you get "1 hour" but if it is one week ago, you get "1 week".

It uses rounding, so the value works out to whole times. However, you can specify a depth so that you end up with better accuracy like "1 week and 3 days ago".

genesis_code($content)

This is a simple function that wraps the content in "<code></code>" tags. It doesn't do a lot, but when you are providing a description in the dashboard, it can be very handy since that will get some nice styling to help it stand out.

genesis_strip_p_tags($content)

This is basically the opposite of the "wpautop()" function. It does exactly what it sounds like. If you have some content that might have paragraphs and you do not want paragraphs, it will take care of the problem no questions asked.

THE GENERAL FUNCTIONS

The general.php file contains several "General" functions. Think of it as "miscellaneous" in that it is more of a catch all for functions that don't really fit anywhere else.

The file has had more and less functions over the years because often a function will end up finding a home once a few other similar functions are created and they all get grouped into a new file.

This does make it somewhat difficult to find specific functions when they are lumped into the catch all, so it is often a good idea to check this file out directly with each update.

Since we are talking "general" functions, this is a great place to explain how you can learn to use new functions. Many plugins and themes do a very poor job with internal documentation. Either functions, classes, and other content exists without a doc block, or it has a very non-descriptive doc block. That is really sad because good internal documentation can not only help users learn to use the plugin or theme, but it will save the developer a lot of headache six months later when they can't remember why they did something the way they did it.

Doc Blocks

In PHP, WordPress, and Genesis, there are several ways of documenting the code. I'm not going to bore you with all the possible ways to do it, but WordPress code standards define a specific way to "do it right". This is because there are tools out there that can convert those docs into helpful information while using certain code editors and with an online parsing tool. It's all very cool and helpful.

Genesis files start with a file doc block. This explains what is in the file. In some cases the information is much better than others. For example, the file docblock for the general.php functions file is:

```
/**
 * Genesis Framework.
 *
 * WARNING: This file is part of the core
Genesis Framework. DO NOT edit this file under
any circumstances.
 * Please do all modifications in the form of a
```

```
child theme.
 *
 * @package Genesis\General
 * @author   StudioPress
 * @license  GPL-2.0+
 * @link     http://my.studiopress.com/themes/
genesis/
 */
```

The "Genesis Framework" doesn't really tell you anything about this file. Fortunately things do get better from there. This does also define some additional information using @ tags, which is part of what makes the doc blocks very helpful.

In this case it specifies the package as "Genesis\General" the author, the license, and a link to the theme.

There are also several function doc blocks found in the file. In fact every single function includes one.

```
/**
 * Enable the author box for ALL users.
 *
 * @since 1.4.1
 *
 * @param array $args Optional. Arguments for
enabling author box. Default is empty array.
 */
```

This one is for the "genesis_enable_author_box" function. It explains what the function does, "Enable the author box for ALL users", when it was added, and what the "$args" parameter is supposed to be.

Learning to read the doc blocks can help you learn new functions more quickly. It also means you can use doc blocks for your own plugin and themes. Even if you will never share the code, it leaves a note for future you. Trust me, future you will thank you for well documented code.

genesis_enable_author_box($args = array())

We just looked at this doc block. In short, add this function to the theme or to a template file in the theme to enable to Genesis author box.

genesis_admin_redirect($page, array $query_args = array())

This does basically what it sounds like. It redirects to a specific admin page. It is possible to include some arguments that will be added to the URL as a query string.

This is not a function you would usually include on the front end of a site. It is generally used when already on the dashboard. It can be used when you change the URL for a settings page or after completing a save action for the options so that a specific admin page with a success or fail message is loaded.

genesis_custom_field_redirect()

This is a callback function that is specifically used to redirect from a custom field value used in Genesis. It's a cool trick you can access even if the Genesis SEO is not enabled on the site due to another SEO plugin running.

In the post/page editor, make sure that the Custom Fields option is enabled in the Screen Options, then add a new field with the name "redirect" and the value as the URL you wish to redirect the post/page to. Then when you go to the post/page URL, it will automatically go to the URL specified.

If you are using Genesis SEO, this option is in the SEO metabox, so it's even easier to use.

genesis_get_theme_support_arg($feature, $arg, $default = '')

This checks to see if the theme supports a given feature. It is mostly helpful when making a plugin that needs to have theme support enabled in the child theme.

In general this is a wrapper for the WordPress function "get_theme_support", but it has some nice additional abilities. This can check for theme support that uses array values to specify different levels of support.

For example, in Genesis it is possible to have support for accessibility with different parts being enabled independently. This function allows checking that support and even having a default to fallback on if the theme doesn't support the expected values.

genesis_detect_plugin(array $plugins)

This is an impressive helper function that can detect if a plugin is active based on the classes, functions, and constants it might have defined. This is very helpful since it is possible to have a plugin installed in a different directory than normally expected.

It is possible to do this logic separately, but this method lets you quickly identify one or more plugins.

```
$args = array(
    'classes' => array(
        'Akismet_Widget',
    ),
);

if ( genesis_detect_plugin( $args ) ) {
    echo 'Akismet is active!';
}
```

The Genesis SEO uses this to deactivate the SEO feature without extensive logic like it used to need because multiple plugins can be checked with a simple array.

genesis_is_menu_page($pagehook = ")

This is another admin function. It checks to see if the current page is the specified page. Working with page hooks can be tricky because the page hook may or may not be defined at the time.

This function has some additional logic to help check for the current page in more than one way.

The function is intended to be used in a conditional statement. It's very helpful, for example, in making sure scripts and styles are loaded on the correct dashboard page and only on that page.

genesis_is_customizer()

This is a simple function that does something WordPress needs because the Customizer is the future. In fact, Genesis settings are moving to use the cCustomizer instead of a separate settings page.

When working on a theme for a client I really prefer to use the Customizer, especially if the settings affect how the site looks. It makes it much easier to make changes and output that to the preview window, but at times code needs to behave one way in preview and a different way when viewing the site.

For example, I'm working on a plugin where it is possible to make design changes in the site. The plugin generates a file with all of the design changes so it doesn't have to rebuild the settings every single page load. This is much more efficient, but it doesn't work well with the Customizer. When using the Customizer, it needs to load the styles it creates in the head.

This function makes it possible to quickly know if the Customizer is being used. You want to know that so the correct version is used to display those style changes and also load the scripts that allow communication between the design window and the settings.

genesis_is_blog_template()

This is another helpful function for conditional statements. WordPress has a function, "is_home()", that identifies if the home page is being used. Some themes call for a static page with a blog page and a separate page using the blog page template with some custom fields that can alter the output. It's really cool, but it is difficult to get the code that targets that specific template. This function makes it easy.

genesis_get_global_post_type_name($post_type_name = ")

This function gets the post type name via two different methods to make it more bulletproof than the WordPress function.

genesis_get_cpt_archive_types()

Mostly this is an internal Genesis function. The main purpose is to get a list of Custom Post Types that have archives. There may be times when a plugin or theme needs this, so it is helpful to know.

Not long ago I was working on a plugin that did need this, and I'm glad Genesis already did the heavy lifting.

genesis_get_cpt_archive_types_names()

This function works with the "genesis_get_cpt_archive_types" function. The main difference is the formatting. The "genesis_get_cpt_archive_types" function will return the post type objects, but this function converts that into a convenient array of names.

genesis_has_post_type_archive_support($post_type_name = ")

This function works with "genesis_get_cpt_archive_types_names". It checks to see if the provided post type name is in the array that "genesis_get_cpt_archive_types_names" returns, then checks to see if it supports the Genesis Archive Settings. It means that you can't use it to check and see if a post type supports archives in general, as it is possible for a post type to have an archive but not have support for the Genesis Archive Settings.

However, if you have a need to know if a post type supports both, then this is the function you need.

genesis_html5()

This is a quick, shorthand function to see if the current theme supports HTML5.

genesis_a11y($arg = 'screen-reader-text')

This checks to see if the current theme supports accessibility; and if an argument is provided, it checks to see if that specific accessibility feature is covered.

This is very helpful in plugins to see if a11y HTML can be output or even better to see if an a11y compatibility style sheet should be loaded so that the plugin can be fully accessible even if the theme is not.

genesis_get_sitemap($heading = 'h2')

This function returns an HTML sitemap. Items are grouped by type like "page" and "post". The groups have a heading that indicates the kind of content that is following. The default heading tag for the group headers is H2. It is possible to override the heading tag in the function arg.

There is a complimentary function "genesis_sitemap" that echos the content immediately without returning it.

genesis_plugin_install_link($plugin_slug = ", $text = ")

This link creates a link to install plugins. This function is very helpful for themes and plugins that need another plugin to be active. It allows notifying a user that the plugin is required. It makes it possible for the user to quickly follow through, without taking the choice away from them, by doing the install and activation under the hood without notifying them.

genesis_is_root_page()

This is another conditional function that makes it easier to identify if the front page of the site is being shown. Depending on the site "settings is_front_page" and "is_home" doesn't always work like expected. This function makes it so that the root page can always be identified regardless of the front page settings.

genesis_canonical_url()

This function returns the canonical URL. This accounts for pagination and the type of page being viewed so author link, archives, and single pages all return the initial canonical URL for that type of content.

WHAT'S NEXT?

We've covered several functions found in the formatting.php and general.php files already. There are quite a few more functions yet to come.

In the next chapter, we will look at image, markup, and options functions. These three files cover a great deal of information, but with the knowledge on how functions are formatted and what a function doc block explains, you are more than ready to conquer those files and build your Genesis expertise.

CHAPTER 11.

GENESIS IMAGE, MARKUP AND OPTIONS FUNCTIONS EXPLAINED

In the previous chapter we covered the formatting.php file and general.php files.

This chapter covers the images.php, markup.php, and options.php files:

- The images.php file is self-explanatory: functions in this file are all about handling images.

- The options.php file deals with WordPress options including post and term meta.

- The markup.php file is more complex and deals with how Genesis can work for XHTML and HTML5 themes as well as some special tricks to allow changing the HTML markup of an element.

If you are browsing the content of the files, you will notice the head.php file was skipped. Those functions are all about the head tag with title and meta fields. Most of them are used for Genesis SEO. So, if the site is using another SEO plugin, those functions are not particularly useful. The exception is the favicon function, which outputs the favicon in the head of the document.

THE IMAGE FUNCTIONS

In this section, we'll go over the following functions in the images.php file:

- **genesis_get_image_id()**: Returns the ID number for an image attached to the post. The First attached image is the default.

- **genesis_get_image()**: Returns attached or featured image per the arguments.

- **genesis_image()**: Echoes "genesis_get_image()".

- **genesis_get_image_sizes()**: Returns array of image sizes.

- **genesis_get_image_sizes_for_customizer()**: Returns an array of images formatted for use in the customizer.

genesis_get_image_id($index = 0, $post_id = null)

This function gets the image attachment ID for a specific post.

By default it will use the current post, and it is possible to get a specific attachment by order.

In general, this is used to get the first image attached to a given post.

genesis_get_image($args = array())

The args are an array, but what does that mean? Well, the short version is you need to send your args as an array. I'll demonstrate that in a minute.

For now, lets look at the defaults.

```
$defaults = array(
'format' => 'html',
'size' => 'full',
'num' => 0,
```

```
'attr' => ''
);
```

This shows four different arguments that can be passed in the array.

1. **format**: This controls the type of information returned.

   - **html** (default): Returns the image formatted for HTML, no need to setup img tags or anything.

   - **url**: Returns a URL for the image. You can use this for a link or to build your own HTML string.

   - **src**: Returns the image "src", which is the image location relative to the index URL. If your image were in "http://example.com/wp-content/uploads/2011/05/img.jpg", then it would return "wp-content/uploads/2011/05/img.jpg".

2. **size**: Controls the size of the image returned based on WordPress image sizes.

   - **full** (default): Returns original image size.

   - **large**: Returns WordPress' large image size.

   - **medium**: Returns WordPress' medium image size.

   - **thumbnail**: Returns WordPress' thumbnail size.

   - **"X"**: Additional image sizes as set with add_image_size(). The name value should be used, not dimensions.

3. **num**: Controls the attached image to return. 0 is the default and will return the first attached image if no featured image is set. Using a value of one or greater will return the second or greater attached image, but will override the featured image.

4. **attr**: This allows you to set the attributes for the img tag returned, set as an array with the attribute as the key and

the attribute values as the string (the example should clarify this).

There are some filters available as well.

- **genesis_get_image_default_args** : This allows you to filter the defaults.
- **genesis_pre_get_image** : This lets you change the args after the args are processed. In other words, it lets you override the args, not just the defaults.
- **genesis_get_image** : This allows you to filter the final returned value.

So here it is in action:

```
$img = genesis_get_image( array(
'format' => 'html',
'size' => 'thumbnail',
'num' => 1,
'attr' => array (
'class' => 'alignleft'
) ) );
```

I could have skipped the format line since that is a default, but I just wanted to show all the values. This will return the thumbnail for the second attached image with class="alignleft".

genesis_image($args = array())

Normally I would just say "this echos 'genesis_get_image()' to save you a bit of code". It does do that, but there is one really nice feature beyond that.

This function will return "false" if there is no image set, so you can do a very simple if/else to return a default image.

```
if( FALSE === genesis_image( array( 'size' =>
```

```
'thumbnail' ) ) )
echo '<img src="http://example.com/
default-image.jpg" />';
```

This will automatically echo the image if it is there. Otherwise, it returns false and that will load the default image.

genesis_get_image_sizes()

This returns an array with all the different image sizes. This is mostly useful in building widgets or setting up theme options where you need to retrieve the available image sizes and pair them with their dimensions. You will have to do a "foreach" when working with it, like this:

```
$image_sizes = genesis_get_image_sizes();

echo '<ul>';
foreach ( $image_sizes as $name => $size ) {
printf ('<li>%s: ( w:%s h:%s )</li>', $name,
$size['width'], $size['height'] );
}
echo '</ul>';
```

This just returns an unordered list of the image sizes with the width and height.

genesis_get_image_sizes_for_customizer()

This is a wrapper for the "genesis_get_image_sizes()" function. The big difference is the image sizes are formatted to be used in an option for the customizer.

The functions for working with images are a little difficult to get used to because you have to work with array values. However, once you do get used to them, you will find they are incredibly flexible and powerful.

THE MARKUP FUNCTIONS

The markup functions comprise an entire file that didn't exist when I first started the Genesis Explained web series. This is fully unique for the book.

The functions found in this file are especially helpful for plugins. Themes can generally use hard coded markup, but plugins needing to support XHTML and HTML5 themes will find these functions invaluable.

Even in a child theme with express support for HTML5, the markup functions can provide access to filters that will help get the correct schema markup in multiple contexts.

Schema is one of those tricky ideas that can help identify content. It is good for search engines to understand the semantic relationships in content. It can also help improve search rankings, but it is not the end all to getting on the first page of Google.

Another good use for schema is accessibility. Correct schema can help identify content to screen readers and make it easier for users with a screen reader to consume content.

Here are the functions found in the genesis/lib/functions/markup.php file

- **genesis_markup()**: Outputs markup conditionally.

- **genesis_xhtml_check()**: Conditionally loads XHTML markup.

- **genesis_parse_attr()**: Merges an array of attributes with defaults.

- **genesis_attr()**: Builds list of attributes into a string and applies contextual filter on string.

- **genesis_attributes_empty_class()**: Makes the class attribute empty.

- **genesis_attributes_screen_reader_class()**: Adds the screen-reader-text class.

- **genesis_skiplinks_markup()**: Adds five additional filters to set skiplink output.

- Callback functions

OK, the last one there might be cheating, but there are over 50 callback functions. They all are very similar, so I'm going to explain the concept there instead of listing over 50 functions.

genesis_markup($args = array())

This is the main function used in this file. The 50 plus callback functions interact with this function. Several other functions exist to support this function. In short, if you can master this function, then everything else falls in line.

The "genesis_markup" function was introduced in Genesis 1.9. The main purpose of the function, at the time, was to start preparing the way for Genesis 2.0 HTML5 support. The idea was there needed to be a way to have a single, authoritative means of setting the markup for all the elements used in the XHTML and HTML5 themes instead of creating two separate sets of structural files that would have to be maintained independently.

The "genesis_markup" function allows generating opening and closing markup for theme elements with the correct attributes using contextually aware options. This means the same function can set the markup for XHTML and HTML5 themes.

It also allows for the markup to be filtered. Previously the markup elements were impossible to change. The heading, nav, body, sidebars, footer and all other elements were hardcoded and had to use the same containers, ids, classes, etc.

This function and the filters it includes allow you to alter the HTML attributes, including the HTML tag for almost every element in the framework output.

Plugins can use this to generate similar HTML5 and XHTML support. You can also use it to make common markup that needs small changes in certain contexts work with a single, authoritative template.

For example, if there is an archive template, taxonomy template, and single template that should all get the same wrappers but with some changes in the ID, class, or other attributes, you can use this function to generate the output. Then you can use a filter to contextually set the required changes.

You can find a good example of how this works in the genesis/lib/structure/xhtml.php file. This file is loaded conditionally if the theme does not support HTML5. It applies filters on markup open and close to ensure the XHTML markup is used instead of the HTML5 markup. This allows the entire framework to use a single source of truth and then modify it only when needed.

genesis_parse_attr($context, $attributes = array(), $args = array())

This is a support function for the "genesis_markup" function. It sets the context as the default class and then merges with the attributes array before running it all through a dynamic filter. The filter is created using the "$context" value.

```
apply_filters( "genesis_attr_{$context}",
$attributes, $context, $args );
```

It is called from inside the genesis_attr function so the attributes can be standardized and filtered.

genesis_attr($context, $attributes = array(), $args = array())

This is another support function for "genesis_markup". This function takes the attributes from the "genesis_markup" function and turns them into a string. So instead of getting an array output for the class, there is a class="classes" output. It uses the "genesis_parse_attr" function to standardize the output and pass it through filters. These filters set classes and other attributes so the output can be contextually modified.

genesis_attributes_empty_class($attributes)

This is a helper function used to make the class empty for a `genesis_attr_{$context}` filter. It's very handy if the markup element shouldn't have any class output because it can be done in one line like:

```
add_filter( 'genesis_attr_child-context',
'genesis_attributes_empty_class' );
```

genesis_attributes_screen_reader_class($attributes)

This is another helper function used to add the ".screen-reader-text" class to an element. This can be very helpful if there are a set of elements that should have screen reader text or should be converted to screen reader text in a specific context.

The screen reader class, if the theme supports it, will make the text not show in the browser but able to be read by a screen reader. This is helpful when there are icons that visually represent what the link/button/element does, but screen readers need a description to replace the visual element.

You can also use it as a single line, like:

```
add_filter( 'genesis_attr_child-context',
'genesis_attributes_screen_reader_class' );
```

THE CALLBACK FUNCTIONS

As I said, there are over 50 callback functions in the markup.php file. They are almost all on the `genesis_attr_{$context}` filter.

Basically, they add additional attributes to the markup of elements using the "$context" to target those elements.

For example:

```
add_filter( 'genesis_attr_head',
'genesis_attributes_head' );
/**
 * Add attributes for head element.
 *
 * @since 2.2.0
 *
 * @param array $attributes Existing attributes
for `head` element.
 * @return array Amended attributes for `head`
element.
 */
 function genesis_attributes_head( $attributes
) {

        $attributes['class'] = '';

        if ( ! is_front_page() ) {
                return $attributes;
        }

        $attributes['itemscope'] = true;
        $attributes['itemtype']    =
'https://schema.org/WebSite';
```

```
        return $attributes;
```

```
}
```

Since these are all callbacks, it is possible to remove those filters with a `remove_filter` and to add your own filter to replace it if desired.

These also provide an excellent example of how to use the dynamic filters to alter the output of the HTML contextually.

OK, now to understand exactly what is happening with this you need a bit of background on schema.

Schema

This is a special HTML markup that tells browsers, search engines, and screen readers what a given part of your code is all about. So if you have a navigation menu, there are some schema elements that are added to that and the search engine, screen reader, and even browser know that it is a menu. If you have your address on the page, you can indicate that it is a place of business address and even your hours of operation using the schema markup.

There are hundreds of schemas and each has a set of possible properties and children. Honestly there is so much going on that there should be a "Schema Explained" book to help clarify all of that.

What you need to know for this is there is an HTML attribute used in schema called itemscope and another called itemtype. If itemscope is "true" then it becomes the parent item to any other schema tags inside of that HTML element. The itemtype defines the actual schema item.

In the code above the itemscope is defined true only on the

front page and the itemscope is defined as a "WebSite." This is "A WebSite is a set of related web pages and other items typically served from a single web domain and accessible via URLs." This is very generic. There are many better schema to use and on some pages those are automatically set to better choices.

However, this becomes tricky because in this case, it is applied to the <head> tag, so the items included in it need to be valid for the scheme selected. It wouldn't be correct to change this value to an "address" when it shows on your about page. Instead the value might be appropriate to use http://schema.org/AboutPage, which indicates the page meta content is referencing the about page.

THE OPTIONS FUNCTIONS

In this section, I'll be going through the genesis/lib/functions/options.php file. There are technically ten functions in the file, but since four of them are just echoing the results of a sister function, there are really only six functions to learn.

Here is the full list of functions:

- genesis_get_option
- genesis_option
- genesis_get_seo_option
- genesis_seo_option
- genesis_get_cpt_option
- genesis_cpt_option
- genesis_custom_field
- genesis_get_custom_field
- genesis_save_custom_fields
- genesis_update_settings

The first four functions deal with theme options and are really some version of "genesis_get_option".

genesis_get_option($key, $setting = null, $use_cache = true)

This function has three possible args.

- The first, "$key", is required. This value indicates which option value to return. For example, if I want to see if the Show Primary Navigation box has been checked, I would use "nav" as my key value. You can look in the genesis/lib/admin/theme-settings.php file for all the built in options.

- The "$setting" value is optional. If it is not defined, and it will look in the "GENESIS_SETTINGS_FIELD". You can also use "GENESIS_SEO_SETTINGS_FIELD" for other built in settings, but those settings can be retrieved more easily with another function, which we'll talk about in a minute. You even have the option of creating your own setting field and retrieving that with this function as well.

- The last, "$user_cache" is a boolean argument. It is true by default and enables the option to be returned from the cache instead of fetching the option. This is a page load cache, so it doesn't last past the current page load, but it can save time when fetching the same option multiple times.

I'll be talking about this in more detail later, including how to add your own options, but for now, lets look at one of the option lines to see how to find the option.

```
<p>
<input
  type="checkbox"
  name="<?php echo GENESIS_SETTINGS_FIELD;
?>[nav]"
  id="<?php echo GENESIS_SETTINGS_FIELD;
?>[nav]"
```

```
  value="1"
  <?php checked(1, genesis_get_option('nav'));
?>
/>
<label for="<?php echo GENESIS_SETTINGS_FIELD;
?>[nav]">
<?php _e("Include Primary Navigation Menu?",
'genesis'); ?>
</label>
</p>
```

Find the name attribute, as that's where you want to look. In this case, it says "GENESIS_SETTINGS_FIELD", so you know what field is being used. Since the function uses that as a default, you don't need to specific the "$setting". I should mention that when you see an all caps bit of code without any quotes, it is called a "constant." This is a special kind of variable that is set using the `define()` function. Like the name implies, a constant is immutable. It cannot be changed or destroyed and all you need to do to access it is type it out. They are usually in all caps to make it easier to identify.

The next part is [nav], and that is your "$key". So, if you want to retrieve the theme option for displaying the navigation, use:

```
$displayNav = genesis_get_option( 'nav' );
```

You can filter the option with "genesis_pre_get_option_'.$key", and the "$key" value means that you can specify which key you are filtering. Thus, if you are trying to change the nav option, you would use:

```
add_filter( 'genesis_pre_get_option_nav',
'child_get_option_nav' );
```

Then you can write a function "child_get_option_nav()" that returns a different value in different circumstances.

Another filter comes just before the value is returned. "genesis_options" lets you filter what is being returned. You could use a "preg_replace" or "str_replace" to change the returned values after they have been retrieved from the database. "genesis_pre_get_option_$key" won't work for that since it returns whatever value you provide instead of checking the database.

"genesis_option()" is exactly the same, except it echos the value.

genesis_get_seo_option($key, $use_cache = true)

This function works mostly the same as "genesis_get_option", except it provides the "GENESIS_SEO_SETTINGS_FIELD" "$setting" value to the "genesis_get_option" function. That saves a bit of code if you are trying to get an SEO setting value. "genesis_seo_option()" just echos the value returned by "genesis_get_seo_option()".

genesis_get_cpt_option($key, $post_type_name = ", $use_cache = true)

This function also uses the "genesis_get_option" function. In the Custom Post Type archive settings, the options are saved to the options table in the database and use the custom post type name as part of the option key. This function simplifies getting the options for any given custom post type.

There is a "genesis_cpt_option()" that is a wrapper for this function to echo the content instead of returning it.

genesis_get_custom_field($field, $post_id = null)

This is another Genesis function that simplifies a WordPress function. The original function only accepted a single argument for the "$field". This was updated a couple of versions ago to allow a second argument for the "$post_id". This argument is optional and will default to the current post id.

To retrieve a custom field inside a Genesis action function, you would need this using the WordPress function:

```
add_action( 'genesis_post_content',
'child_custom_field' );
function child_custom_field() {
global $post;

$myField = get_post_meta( $post->ID,
'field_name', true );

echo $myField;
}
```

Using Genesis functions, you could simplify that to:

```
add_action( 'genesis_post_content',
'child_custom_field' );
function child_custom_field() {
    genesis_custom_field( 'field_name' );
}
```

There are times you wouldn't use this function. It won't work with array values, so if you have multiple fields with the same name, you need to use WordPress functions to retrieve an object (array) that you can then convert into strings you will be able to output.

The function also has some built in safety checks that can prevent some code from working right. It runs the "stripslashes()" function and "wp_kses_decode_entities()" function before returning a value. Most of the time this isn't an issue, and the "genesis_get_custom_field()" function is a huge time saver.

The "genesis_custom_field()" function echos this value automatically but has a new feature for "$output_pattern".

```
genesis_custom_field( $field, $output_pattern = '%s', $post_id = null )
```

The output pattern uses printf so the content can be put in context if there is a value. This is very helpful since it will not output the context with an empty value.

```
genesis_custom_field( 'my-custom-field', __( 'Here is the value: %s', 'child' ) )
```

If there is a value for my-custom-field, then it will output as "here is the value: value". However, if there is no value, then nothing gets output.

genesis_save_custom_fields(array $data, $nonce_action, $nonce_name, $post, $deprecated = null)

This is a helper function that does a lot of the custom field save logic for you. If you are using a theme or plugin to add custom meta boxes to a post editor, then this can simplify the save action.

```
add_action( 'save_post', 'child_save_post', 10, 2 );
/**
 * My save post action.
 *
 * @param int      $post_id Post ID of the post
being saved.
 * @param WP_Post $post     The post object
being saved.
 */
```

```
function child_save_post( $post_id, $post ) {
    if ( 'my_post_type' !== $post->post_type ) {
        return;
    }

    $custom_fields = array(
        'my_custom_field' => empty(
$_POST['my_custom_field'] ) ? '' :
$_POST['my_custom_field'],
    );

    genesis_save_custom_fields( $custom_fields,
'my_nonce_action', 'my_nonce_name', $post );
}
```

This has a bit of logic to make sure the post is a specific custom post type, and it sets up the data that will be saved. At this point, the data could go through some sanitization to ensure it is safe when saved.

The nonce action is the key used to create the nonce value. The nonce name is the name value on the hidden nonce input. It will check the "$_POST" array for that key value when checking the nonce.

The function will verify the nonce, make sure it is not an autosave, ajax request, cron request, or revision. Then it will update the post meta if the value exists, or it will delete the post meta if the value does not exist.

These are common steps taken in a save post, so this can save a lot of code.

genesis_update_settings($new = ", $setting = GENESIS_SETTINGS_FIELD)

This helper function makes it easy to update an array settings where the existing settings are preserved if the new settings do not have that specific setting.

A good use case for this is when you are using the "GENESIS_SETTINGS_FIELD" for the setting and updating only the settings for the plugin or child theme. There are a LOT of other settings in that array that can come from Genesis, another plugin, or even a different part of the child theme. This does the logic to ensure those other settings are preserved and only the settings that should be altered are affected.

WHAT'S NEXT?

This was a lot of information, and I nearly fell down the rabbit hole when we got to schema. At this point you have covered the image, markup, and option functions and even got a quick primer on schema.

The next chapter will cover the widgetize and layout functions. There is a lot of information there, especially with understanding how sidebars and widget areas work. We'll see how they can be simplified with Genesis and then look at how the entire page layout system works.

CHAPTER 12.

GENESIS WIDGETIZE AND LAYOUT FUNCTIONS EXPLAINED

The last chapter was about the image, markup and options functions and demonstrated some very important functions for retrieving custom fields and theme options from the database.

This chapter is all about the genesis/lib/functions/widgetize.php file and the genesis/lib/functions/layout.php file.

So get ready to learn about the difference between sidebars and widget areas, how they work in the Genesis theme, and how layout functions control the overall layout of each page of the site as well the the settings for those pages.

THE WIDGETIZE FUNCTIONS

There are really only a few functions you will be using in the theme, but you can also learn a lot of useful functions from this file.

Here is a list of all the functions in the file.

- **genesis_register_widget_area()**: Registers a widget area.

- **genesis_register_sidebar()**: Registers new sidebars (uses "genesis_register_widget_area").

- **genesis_register_default_widget_areas()**: This is part of an action hook and temporarily registers the default widget areas.

- **_genesis_register_default_widget_areas_cb()**: This is a callback for default widget areas to permanently register defaults that have not been removed.

- **genesis_register_footer_widget_areas:** This is part of an action hook and registers the footer widget areas.

- **genesis_register_after_entry_widget_area()**: This is part of an action hook and registers the after post widget areas.

- **genesis_widget_area()**: This conditionally displays the dynamic sidebar.

- **genesis_a11y_register_sidebar_defaults()**: Sets accessibility defaults if supported.

- **genesis_sidebar_title()**: Adds semantic and accessible aware headings to the sidebar.

Before we dive into that, though, I want to talk about some terms.

Sidebar

A sidebar is the WordPress term for any part of the theme that widgets can be added to. Widgets were normally relegated to "sidebars", so that is why this term is used. However, more and more advanced themes make use of all parts of the theme for widgets. So WordPress developers use both terms interchangeably: "sidebars" and "widget areas".

A sidebar has several important parts. The sidebar name, ID, before and after widget, and before and after widget title. We'll talk about these in more details later.

The term sidebar is mostly replaced with widget area in Genesis, so it is less confusing than it used to be, but look for the terms to be somewhat interchangeable in older functions.

Widget

Widgets go into sidebars. Widgets are registered in WordPress using a special class extender and have two main parts: the back end and the front end. On the back end, you can drag widgets into sidebars. You can also set the widget settings once they are in the sidebar. If a widget can't find its home, it goes to the inactive widgets. This happens when the ID changes. Again, I'll talk about this more later. The front end is what actually appears on the site.

genesis_register_widget_area($args)

This function registers a new widget area. The function "genesis_register_sidebar()" is an old function that preceded this one and is now a wrapper for this function.

This function has a single arg, but it is an array value. There are defaults built in:

```
$defaults = array(
    'before_widget' => genesis_markup( array(
        'open'      => '<section id="%%1$s"
class="widget %%2$s"><div class="widget-wrap">',
        'context' => 'widget-wrap',
        'echo'      => false,
    ) ),
    'after_widget'  => genesis_markup( array(
        'close'     => '</div></section>' . "\n",
        'context' => 'widget-wrap',
        'echo'      => false,
    ) ),
    'before_title'  => '<h4 class="widget-title
widgettitle">',
    'after_title'   => "</h4>\n",
);
```

There are two filters available to modify these defaults:

"genesis_register_sidebar_defaults"   and
"genesis_register_widget_area_defaults". They do the same thing
with the only difference being the newer filter adopts the "widget
area" terminology.

These are very handy if you want a different title or widget
wrap. Once the defaults are parsed with the arguments that are
passed, a new sidebar is registered with the WordPress function
"register_sidebar()". Of course you could just use that function,
but look how much more efficient the Genesis function is.

```
//WordPress Function
register_sidebar( array(
    'name'            => __( 'My Sidebar', 'child'
),
    'id'              => 'my-sidebar',
    'before_widget' => genesis_markup( array(
        'open'     => '<section id="%1$s"
class="widget %%2$s"><div class="widget-wrap">',
        'context' => 'widget-wrap',
        'echo'     => false,
    ) ),
    'after_widget'  => genesis_markup( array(
        'close'    => '</div></section>' . "\n",
        'context' => 'widget-wrap',
        'echo'     => false,
    ) ),
    'before_title'  => '<h4 class="widget-title
widgettitle">',
    'after_title'   => "</h4>\n",
) );

//Genesis Function
genesis_register_widget_area(
    array (
        'name' => __( 'My Sidebar', 'child' ),
```

```
      'id'    => 'my-sidebar',
) );
```

Each of these will create identical sidebars, but you need much less information with the genesis function. The only requirements are the name and id. If you want, you can even skip the ID, but I don't recommend it. If you have a properly formed ID, then your widgets will stay at home where they belong. Otherwise, if there is a change in the order of the sidebars, then your widgets will move to other sidebars or into the inactive widgets.

An ID should be lowercase and have no spaces. If you want to use a space, then put a "-" in there. This is important because the ID is used as an html ID, so you need to conform to html standards. Plus, if you have spaces, WordPress can lose track of your widgets.

Of course, if you want to create a special sidebar with a different widget wrap and title wrap, you can change the defaults.

You can remove any of the default sidebars by unregistering them. This is done with the WordPress "unregister_sidebar()" function. Just put this in your functions.php file to get rid of the secondary sidebar:

```
unregister_sidebar( 'sidebar-alt' );
```

Of course this still leaves the layout options in place. To get rid of them, you need to remove layout options. The next section will cover the layout.php file with the functions that remove or add layouts.

genesis_widget_area($id, $args = array())

I contributed to this function to solve a particular issue. In WordPress, a sidebar can have content or not have content. It is possible to use some functions to dynamically show default content, and it is pretty powerful. However, it is also somewhat clunky if the idea is to just show the sidebar if and only if there are widgets to display.

This function simplifies the process of showing the sidebar with the appropriate markup around it, and it is possible to show it only if there are widgets in the sidebar. It also adds the ability to alter the defaults with the "genesis_widget_area_defaults" filter.

For most uses, you can display a dynamic sidebar with default markup using a simple, single argument function like this:

```
genesis_widget_area ( 'widget-area-id' );
```

This will use the default HTML and is pretty magical, but the real magic is that this function will return a boolean. So, it is still possible to add default output. In fact, it is easier than the WordPress function because it takes less code.

```
if ( ! genesis_widget_area ( 'widget-area-id' )
) {
    // Do your default here.

}
```

Compared to the old method, this is the kind of magic that will get underaged wizards in big trouble.

THE LAYOUT FUNCTIONS

In this section, I'm going to be going through the genesis/lib/ functions/layout.php file. I intentionally went out of order with this because it is helpful to be familiar with the concept of sidebars and the functions Genesis uses regarding them before trying to understand layouts.

There are 20 functions in the file and only one is part of an existing hook. The rest involve creating, removing, and checking layout options.

This is very helpful in working with Genesis since you can select layouts for individual posts, pages, and terms. This means you can create whole new layouts without resorting to templates.

Let's look at the layout functions:

- **genesis_create_initial_layouts()**: Registers the default layouts.

- **genesis_register_layout()**: Registers a single layout.

- **genesis_add_type_to_layout()**: Adds a new type to the layout type arguments.

- **genesis_remove_type_from_layout()**: Removes a type from the layout type arguments.

- **genesis_set_default_layout()**: Sets the default layout for a theme.

- **genesis_unregister_layout()**: Removes a registered layout.

- **genesis_get_layouts()**: Gets an array of layouts.

- **genesis_get_layouts_for_customizer()**: Gets an array of layouts formatted for the customizer options.

- **genesis_get_layout()**: Gets a specific layout including arguments.

- **genesis_get_default_layout()**: Gets the default layout.

- **genesis_has_multiple_layouts()**: Determines if there is more than one registered layout.

- **genesis_site_layout()**: Gets the page layout based on the context.

- **genesis_layout_selector()**: Outputs the layout selector.

- **genesis_structural_wrap()**: Outputs structural wraps if they are supported for the context.
- The following return the layout ID for the specified layout:

  - **__genesis_return_content_sidebar()**: content-sidebar

  - **__genesis_return_sidebar_content()**: sidebar-content

  - **__genesis_return_content_sidebar_sidebar()**: content-sidebar-sidebar

  - **__genesis_return_sidebar_sidebar_content()**: sidebar-sidebar-content

  - **__genesis_return_sidebar_content_sidebar()**: sidebar-content-sidebar

  - **__genesis_return_full_width_content()**: full-width-content

Now there are a fair number of functions there. Most themes and plugins won't use these, but it is helpful to know a few of them. Some are also helpful for advanced usage, like registering additional layouts.

genesis_create_initial_layouts()

This is a callback function used to register the default layouts. It isn't something used in a theme or plugin, but there is a helpful filter that lets a theme or plugin change the default layouts before they are even registered.

```
add_filter( 'genesis_initial_layouts',
'child_initial_layouts' );
/**
 * Filter to remove the default layouts not
used in this theme.
 *
 * @param array $default_layouts The default
```

```
layouts.
 *
 * @return array
 */
function child_initial_layouts(
$default_layouts ) {
    unset(
$default_layouts['content-sidebar-sidebar'] );
    unset(
$default_layouts['sidebar-sidebar-content'] );
    unset(
$default_layouts['sidebar-content-sidebar'] );

    return $default_layouts;
}
```

The trick here is to make sure the filter is registered *before* the "genesis_setup" action, or it will not work.

genesis_register_layout($id = ", $args = array())

This is how you register a new layout. The ID and args are *optional*, but if they are not specified, it will not do anything. It will just fail silently.

The args accept three keyed values:

```
$args = array(
    'label' => '(Internationalized name of the
layout)',
    'img'   => '(URL path to layout image)',
    'type'  => '(Layout type)',
);
```

The label and image are pretty straight forward.

The layout is what shows for the name of the layout.

The image is used where an image can represent the layout.

Type is a contextual value. Most of the time this can be skipped or set to the default of 'site'. There are instances where a specific context is used for a layout, but this is generally done when registering a whole new type of layout.

For example, if a theme were to generate a set of layouts for a specific post type, those layouts could be registered with the post type name as the type, and custom archive and post editor settings could be created using the available functions. Then the layout can be limited to only that type. It's a pretty advanced usage, and most of the time it is best to use 'site' to keep it simple.

genesis_add_type_to_layout($id, $type = array())

This and the sister function, "genesis_remove_type_from_layout()", work to modify the type argument for the layouts. It is a very advanced usage, so don't feel bad if it isn't clear right off the bat.

Like the previous example, it is possible to create a type that is used in a specific section of the site. Then it may be desired to have existing layouts work with that type instead of registering each of them. For example, you may wish to have the full width layout option available. Then you could use the code:

```
genesis_add_type_to_layout(
'full-width-content', array( 'child_cpt_type' )
);
```

The "genesis_remove_type_from_layout" works the same way but removes the layout from the types specified.

genesis_set_default_layout($id = ")

When making a child theme, it may be preferable to have a

specific layout active if no other layout is selected. This is the function you would use to make that happen.

genesis_unregister_layout($id = ")

If you don't use the filter to remove layouts, this is how you can remove them easily with a simple function.

```
genesis_unregister_layout(
'content-sidebar-sidebar' );
```

genesis_get_layouts($type = 'site')

This function gets an array of layouts. By default, it gets the 'site' layouts, but it is possible to specify a type. This is an advanced usage, but it can be helpful with advanced custom post types, taxonomies, or other layouts that should behave differently from the site layout with a completely different set of layout options.

genesis_get_layouts_for_customizer($type = 'site')

This works just like the "genesis_get_layouts" function and even uses that function. The difference is the array returned is formatted for use in the customizer options.

genesis_get_layout($id, $type = 'site')

This returns the layout with the arguments. It is type aware. This does not depend on the settings. It can be helpful to find out a specific layout label or to take the layout settings when registering a new layout with a different type. However, there is a function to add a type to an existing layout, which is a much better approach.

genesis_get_default_layout($type = 'site')

This returns the default layout even if there is a setting or context option that would override it. This accepts the type argument, but the "genesis_set_default_layout()" does not currently access the type argument. The only way to use the default layout with the "$type" argument is to use the hidden arg key value 'default' when registering a layout for a specific type. In general, this is not the intended usage and runs the risk of causing problems, unlike with the "genesis_set_default_layout()" function. However, if you need a default layout for a specific type, then that is the only way to do it for now.

genesis_has_multiple_layouts($type = 'site')

This is a simple function that returns true if there is more than one registered layout. It is used in Genesis to optionally hide the layout settings when all other layouts have been removed.

genesis_site_layout($use_cache = true)

This function gets the layout. It uses context to identify overriding settings. So, if on a single page, it first checks the page meta to see if the layout was set on the page, it then checks the theme/customizer settings to see if there is a layout setting. Finally, it falls back to the default layout.

There is also a filter, "genesis_site_layout", at the top of the function that can set a specific layout before the function does anything else. This can be very helpful when a specific layout is needed for a given custom post type or page template.

There are some helpful functions that can make this very easy.

- __genesis_return_content_sidebar(): content-sidebar
- __genesis_return_sidebar_content(): sidebar-content
- __genesis_return_content_sidebar_sidebar(): content-sidebar-sidebar
- __genesis_return_sidebar_sidebar_content(): sidebar-sidebar-content

- __genesis_return_sidebar_content_sidebar(): sidebar-content-sidebar

- __genesis_return_full_width_content(): full-width-content

So, if you have a template that must be full width and does not support any other layout, you can bypass all settings with one line of code in the template before the "genesis()" line:

```
add_filter( 'genesis_site_layout',
'__genesis_return_full_width_content' );
```

This will force full width content automatically. How cool is that?

genesis_layout_selector($args = array())

This is the function Genesis uses to output the layout settings. The args can specify:

```
$args = array(
    'name'     => 'the html name value',
    'selected' => 'the current selected value',
    'echo'     => 'true to echo false to
return',
    'type'     => 'default is site but other
types can be specified',
);
```

genesis_structural_wrap($context = ", $output = 'open', $echo = true)

This is used to generate structural wraps for specific elements. It is helpful to get the same HTML markup to open and close the element. The context sets specific classes used in the theme, and there are new markups that are automatically mapped to replace old markup for elements like the menus and inner wrap.

This function is mostly an internal function that isn't generally used in a child theme or plugin. Most often child themes would use specific wraps as needed without needing this function. There are some cases where a plugin might be recreating the structural wrap elements and need to be contextually aware for new and old HTML markup. The markup formatting can get somewhat complex when accounting for the XHTML and HTML5 theme support, so this and other markup functions can simplify that to some degree.

WHAT'S NEXT?

Now that you know how to register and deregister widget areas and layouts, as well as control how and when they display, you are ready to move on.

We have not covered every single function, but we have gone over the main functions used in plugins and themes. More importantly, we have covered how functions work and where to find the information you need to understand and use the functions in Genesis.

The next chapters deal with classes. This can be a difficult topic, even for experienced WordPress developers. The following chapter will explain several basic concepts about classes and give an overview of the history of classes in Genesis as well as the class files.

CHAPTER 13.

GENESIS CLASSES EXPLAINED

In my twenties, I worked in construction. I loved demolition, but also got pretty good at rough carpentry, finish carpentry, drywall, roofing, and even concrete. During that time, I learned there is a right tool for every job.

Have you ever heard the saying, "If the only tool you have is a hammer, pretty soon everything starts to look like a nail"?

Whether you're working in construction, or as a WordPress developer, it is tempting to take the same approach all the time.

In the WordPress world, a lot of developers are afraid of classes so they only ever use static functions. Just like the person with only a hammer, they believe that the best tool for any job is the static function. In this chapter, my goal is to convince you that classes are the right tool for many tasks.

WHAT ARE CLASSES?

Classes are the backbone for an approach to coding called "Object-oriented programming".

At first, you might think the name should be "Class-oriented Programing." However, when you use a class you are really using the object rather than the class. One class can become multiple objects. While the classes and objects start exactly the same, as you work with them, they can become different.

This is difficult to explain, but easy to show. Let's say we have a class called "Person":

```
class Person {

    /**
     * The first name.
     *
     * @param string
     */
    var $first_name = '';

    /**
     * The last name.
     *
     * @param string
     */
    var $last_name = '';

    /**
     * Constructor for the Person class.
     */
    public function __construct( $first_name,
$last_name ) {

        $this->first_name = $first_name;
        $this->last_name  = $last_name;

    }

    /**
     * Gets the specified property.
     *
```

```
    * @param string $property The property to
get.
    *
    * @returns mixed|string|bool
    public function get( $property ) {
        return empty( $this->$property ) ?
false : $this->$property;
    }
}
```

This is a pretty simple class as classes go, but it does work really well to help explain what an object is.

The code above is the class, which defines some properties and methods.

- **Properties**: The variables at the top of the class.
- **Methods**: The functions that make up the class.

When instantiating the class, you specify the person's first and last name like this:

```
$person_1 = new Person( 'Nick', 'Croft' );
$person_2 = new Person( 'John', 'Smith' );
$person_3 = new Person( 'Jane', 'Doe' );
```

Now there are three objects, "$person_1", "$person_2", and "$person_3". This lets us get information about those "Persons" using the get method.

For example, let's say I want to build a table about these three people.

```
<table>
    <thead>
        <tr>
            <th>First Name</th>
```

```
        <th>Last Name</th>
      </tr>
    </thead>
    <tbody>
      <tr>
        <td><?php echo $person_1->get( 'firs
t_name' ); ?></td>
        <td><?php echo $person_1->get( 'last
_name' ); ?></td>
      </tr>
      <tr>
        <td><?php echo $person_2->get( 'firs
t_name' ); ?></td>
        <td><?php echo $person_2->get( 'last
_name' ); ?></td>
      </tr>
      <tr>
        <td><?php echo $person_3->get( 'firs
t_name' ); ?></td>
        <td><?php echo $person_3->get( 'last
_name' ); ?></td>
      </tr>
    </tbody>
</table>
```

This could be done with a function and some complicated global arrays, but this is a great example where an object is really the best tool for the job.

CLASS HISTORY IN GENESIS

Now that you have some background on classes, let's look at the history of classes in Genesis.

When the framework first came out, there were no classes. In some ways, things were easier. There was a lot to learn with abstracted development, so learning OOP would have really been a struggle.

The breadcrumb class was the first to be added, and then the admin class came along. In behind-the-scenes discussion, there has been a push for more and more classes. This is a very positive move because it points to the care in the development of Genesis. This means that thoughtful developers are pushing for modern PHP but understand that the framework needs to be easier for new developers. Just like how static functions aren't the only and best tool, classes also have their place and limitations.

CLASSES IN GENESIS

Right now, there are eleven classes in eight files in the classes directory.

Four of the classes follow the WordPress coding standard for naming files class-{lowercase-separated-classname}.php.

There are also some additional classes found in the admin directory, which are an extension of the Genesis Admin classes. We'll look at these in more detail later in the Admin chapters of this book.

That is a fair bit of growth, and there are likely to be additional classes in the future.

Also there is a push to correctly name all of the class files and pull individual classes into their own files, which fits with the coding standards.

For now the files are:

- **admin.php**: Contains four admin classes used to build dashboard pages.
- **breadcrumb.php**: Contains the breadcrumb class used to generate the breadcrumb output.

- **class-genesis-admin-meta-boxes.php**: One of the admin classes.

- **class-genesis-contributor.php**: Creates the contributor object for outputting details on the contributor page in the dashboard.

- **class-genesis-contributors.php**: Creates the contributors object which stores and iterates multiple contributor objects.

- **class-genesis-script-loader.php**: Registers and enqueues multiple scripts used in the dashboard and front end of the site.

- **cli.php**: Registers a WP CLI callback function that is used for upgrading networks without logging into every site.

- **sanitization.php**: Handles the sanitization of options when they are saved.

Since I'll be talking in-depth on the admin section in later chapters, I will discuss those classes in that part of the book. Also, the contributor, contributors, and CLI classes are not generally used outside of the Genesis core, so I will skip those for now.

WHAT'S NEXT?

In the following chapters, we'll look at the breadcrumb, meta boxes, script-loader, and sanitization classes in more details.

We'll also look at using filters and actions with classes. This is important because there are some special considerations with that use case.

CHAPTER 14.

GENESIS BREADCRUMB AND META BOXES CLASSES EXPLAINED

The first class to be added to Genesis was Breadcrumb Class.

I vividly remember when this change was first proposed. I hated the idea.

Classes were different. I had worked with objects before, but mostly I didn't really understand **why** anyone would use them. It felt like adding one more layer on top of an already complicated and abstract code base.

I wasn't the only one to feel this way. A lot of other developers also pushed back. However, all the work was already done, so classes were included as a kind of experiment. The Genesis team wanted to see if classes could resolve some of the difficulties the framework had with breadcrumbs. They also wanted to see how developers reacted to a class being used in a theme when that was far from normal.

In the past several years, I've grown much more fond of classes and often plan new projects around them. I find that an object holding the state of a particular page is much more efficient in terms of code and processing. Additionally, well formed classes are actually relatively easy to understand and use, once you get past the initial learning curve.

Previously, we covered a brief overview of classes, the history in Genesis, and the class files in Genesis. This chapter will give some more information on class structure as well as looking at two key classes in Genesis. The Breadcrumb class is the oldest class, and the metaboxes class is one of the newest.

UNDERSTANDING CLASS STRUCTURE

Before getting into these classes, it is helpful to know a bit more about how class structure works.

In the previous chapter, I mentioned there are properties and methods. The property is a variable that exists in the scope of the class. Often these appear at the top of a class, before the methods. Methods are functions inside the class.

Each property and method can have one of three possible access levels: public, protected, and private. This is very important to know because it affects how you interact with the class and the properties/methods.

- **Public**: Can be accessed outside the class.
- **Protected**: Can be accessed only by the class or a subclass that is extending the class.
- **Private**: Can be accessed only by the class.

These are very important to maintain the integrity of the object.

Let's look at the example of the Person class from the prior chapter. If we could make the properties private, then it wouldn't be possible to change them, unless there is a method that lets you make that change.

```
class Person {

    /**
     * The first name.
```

```php
     *
     * @param string
     */
    private $first_name = '';

    /**
     * The last name.
     *
     * @param string
     */
    private $last_name = '';

    /**
     * Constructor for the Person class.
     */
    public function __construct( $first_name,
$last_name ) {

        $this->first_name = $first_name;
        $this->last_name  = $last_name;

    }

    /**
     * Gets the specified property.
     *
     * @param string $property The property to
get.
     *
     * @returns mixed|string|bool
    public function get( $property ) {
        return empty( $this->$property ) ?
false : $this->$property;
    }
}
```

By doing this, you will know that the first name, last name, and any other property will always be what they were created to be and nothing could accidentally change it. If someone tried with some code like "$person_1->first_name = 'Bob' ;", then there would be an error.

It also means something can't maliciously change your object, which improves the security of the object.

If that was a protected property, then it would be possible to extend the Person class to make a Doctor class that is used to alter the output just a bit.

```
class Doctor extends Person {

    /**
     * Gets the specified property.
     *
     * @param string $property The property to
get.
     *
     * @returns mixed|string|bool
    public function get( $property ) {

        switch ( $property ) {
            case 'name':
                // Translators: The
placeholders are for the first and last name
values respectively.
                $value = sprintf( __( 'Dr. %s
%s', 'child' ), $this->first_name,
$this->last_name );
                break;
            case 'last_name':
                // Translators: The placeholder
is for the last name.
```

```
            $value = sprintf( __( 'Dr. %s',
'child' ), $this->last_name );
                break;
            default:
                $value = empty(
$this->$property ) ? false : $this->$property;
        }
        return $value;
    }
}
```

As you can see, by extending the Person class, you don't have to repeat everything in the Doctor class. All you need to do is replace the method that should be different. You can add additional methods and properties as well, but you can't make something that is protected or private public. Those states are immutable.

THE BREADCRUMB CLASS

Now that you have an understanding on how classes work and what an object is, it'll be much easier to look at the breadcrumb.php file to see what is happening and how it can affect a theme.

In addition to the class file, there is also a function file named breadcrumb.php. That file does the heavy lifting while conditionally invoking the Genesis breadcrumb class, another plugin breadcrumb, or no breadcrumb. It all depends on the setting and plugins that might be active.

GENESIS_BREADCRUMB

The Genesis Breadcrumb class has three public methods. Everything else is protected. This means you are limited on what you can get from the object. When you instantiate it with "new Genesis_Breadcrumb();", it will generate the basic output using the default args. However, the constructor method does not accept any arguments. So, if you wish to alter the default args, you must use the "genesis_breadcrumb_args" filter. Nearly every method has a filter, so you can alter the output with a total of 22 possible filters, which is enough to do almost anything you want without difficulty.

However, if you need to do something more, then the only option is to extend the class and replace methods or add new methods. This will give you access to all of the properties and methods directly. It is important to note that extending the class will not automatically replace it.

You will have to replace the default breadcrumb action with your own action and replace the "genesis_breadcrumb" function with your own function that instantiates your breadcrumb.

When you use a class it opens the door to building the content and modifying it with filters. This is much more powerful than the static functions which were previously used. Additionally, the code becomes more self contained and testable, which also solves other problems and makes it easier to modify without breaking things.

THE META BOXES CLASS

Genesis_Admin_Meta_Boxes is one of the newest class in Genesis. It was added in Genesis 2.5 and creates metaboxes for use with the "Genesis_Admin_Boxes" class. It is helpful to look at it compared to the breadcrumbs class to see the evolution of classes in Genesis. It should be noted, however, that you may feel more comfortable understanding what is happening here after looking at the chapters about the Admin class. It is similar to and different from the admin classes so if you have trouble, circle back to this again to see if a different perspective is helpful to understanding what is happening in this class.

Unlike other admin classes, this is specialized as a reusable object for adding metaboxes to various pages.

In the admin folder, it is used in the inpost-metaboxes.php, term-meta.php, and user-meta.php files to add meta boxes to those pages.

It is effective for displaying the views output for various metaboxes.

NO CREATE IN THE META BOXES CLASS

Unlike other admin classes, this does not make use of the "create()" method to add a menu item and admin page. Instead the "_construct" method sets the "help_base" and "views_base" properties.

```
public function __construct() {

                $this->help_base   =
GENESIS_VIEWS_DIR . '/help/';
                $this->views_base =
GENESIS_VIEWS_DIR;


        }
```

show_meta_box($id, $object = null)

This is the main method used. It is accessed via the "genesis_meta_boxes()" function. If you remember, this function returns a static instance of the "Genesis_Admin_Meta_Boxes" object, which makes it very easy to interact with this method.

However, there is a big limitation, this method works with the "help_base" and "views_base" properties that were set when this object was created. So, it is limited to the Genesis views directory, and there isn't a way around that.

However, it is still possible to use the class to make a new object that will work in a child theme or plugin.

```php
/**
 * Register meta boxes added to WordPress admin
screens.
 *
 * @package Child\Admin
 */
class Child_Admin_Meta_Boxes extends
Genesis_Admin_Meta_Boxes {

        /**
         * Create a meta box handler.
         *
         * @since 2.5.0
         */
        public function __construct() {

                // Use these for a child theme.
                $this->help_base  =
get_stylesheet_directory() . '/lib/views/help/';
                $this->views_base =
get_stylesheet_directory() . '/lib/views/';

                /* Use these for a plugin.
                $this->help_base  =
MY_GENESIS_PLUGIN_DIR . '/lib/views/help/';
                $this->views_base =
MY_GENESIS_PLUGIN_DIR . '/lib/views/';
                /**/
        }

}
```

```
/**
 * Handle for Child_Admin_Meta_Boxes class.
 *
 * @since 2.5.0
 */
function child_meta_boxes() {

        static $meta_boxes = null;

        if ( null === $meta_boxes ) {
                $meta_boxes = new
Child_Admin_Meta_Boxes();
        }

        return $meta_boxes;

}
```

With this you could use the views directory to add meta boxes to any page just like Genesis is doing.

WHAT'S NEXT?

I have to admit, my introduction to classes and object oriented programing took several weeks. I went through the breadcrumbs class and asked Gary Jones, the author of the class, several questions. Then when the admin classes came out, I was able to follow along and better understand what was happening. It's been years now and I feel more than comfortable around Object-oriented programming.

With the information you have about classes, objects, the Genesis class structure, plus the Breadcrumbs and Metabox classes, you are well on your way.

The next chapter will cover the Sanitization and Script Loader classes. These are helpful for working with admin pages by making submitted content safe for the database and ensuring you have the scripts you need when you need them.

CHAPTER 15.

GENESIS SANITIZATION AND SCRIPT LOADER CLASSES EXPLAINED

This chapter continues to build on the knowledge you have about classes.

The sanitizer class will explain what sanitization is, how to register new options for the sanitizer, and gives additional information about class structure that will be helpful to understanding object oriented programing.

Then the script loader will be a welcome break from Object-oriented programming (OOP). The best part about working with the script loader class is you don't need to directly use classes or objects to take advantage of this class.

THE SANITIZER CLASS

Before explaining the Sanitizer class, let's start with a more basic question: "What is Sanitization?"

To understand Sanitization, it's helpful to think about it in the context of security. There are three basic methods of securing data:

- Validation
- Sanitization

- Escaping

Generally speaking, you want to validate and sanitize early, then escape late.

In short, don't trust anything. 99.99% of your users are probably perfectly innocent, but it just takes one user to ruin your whole year.

What is Validation? Validation ensures that the data you are getting is the right kind of data. It's super helpful to do this on the client level and can be very good for users because it can catch accidents and not just malicious intent. For example, if you have a contact form on the site with an email address field, you can validate that as an email address. This will return an error and let the user know there was a problem with the email address if they forget the "@" or some other part of the email address. You can even attach this to email validation services, which can verify the domain is connected to an email server and otherwise ensure it is a good email address. The email validation services can also make suggestions if there is a typo that can save your users a lot of hassle, but that won't protect your database.

What is Sanitization? It is possible to bypass Validation and send information directly to the server. If you are saving the input to the database, you want to make sure the data is safe so that you can sanitize the data. This will strip content that doesn't fit with the data type.

What is Escaping? If you are going to display this your data, you need to escape it. Escaping will convert characters into formats that are acceptable for the context where they will appear. Escaping can be very helpful, even with content that you trust. For example, if you have a link to tweet your post with the post title, twitter handle, and a hashtag, you can use the correct character conversion and escaping to ensure the URL is formatted correctly. Otherwise, the link will mess up at the first space instead of correctly joining the entire title with all the other parts you are including.

WHAT IS STATIC?

Static is another OOP concept and keyword you will see in classes. It doesn't alter the availability of the method or property like the public, protected, and private keywords. It can also work with those keywords so it is alongside them.

Static is a keyword used in functional PHP, which is similar but different, so that makes it even more confusing.

The simplest explanation is a static method or property can be used without creating the object. This is convenient, but it also means that the static method doesn't have access to the object. If you try to use "$this" inside a static method, you will get an error.

Let's look at an example from the Person class.

```php
class Person {

    /**
     * The first name.
     *
     * @param string
     */
    var $first_name = '';

    /**
     * The last name.
     *
     * @param string
     */
    var $last_name = '';
```

```php
    /**
     * Prefix used to identify the Person.
     *
     * @param string
     */
    static $prefix = '';

    /**
     * Constructor for the Person class.
     */
    public function __construct( $first_name,
$last_name ) {

        $this->first_name = $first_name;
        $this->last_name  = $last_name;

    }

    /**
     * Gets the specified property.
     *
     * @param string $property The property to
get.
     *
     * @returns mixed|string|bool
    public function get( $property ) {

        switch ( $property ) {
            case 'name':
                // Translators: The
placeholders are for the prefix, first name,
and last name values respectively.
                $value = sprintf( __( '%1$s%2$s
%3$s', 'child' ), Person::get_prefix(),
$this->first_name, $this->last_name );
```

```php
                break;
            case 'last_name':
                // Translators: The placeholder
is for the prefix and last name.
                $value = sprintf( __(
'%1$%2$s', 'child' ), $this->last_name );
                break;
            default:
                $value = empty(
$this->$property ) ? false : $this->$property;
        }
        return $value;
    }


    /**
     * Gets the static $prefix property.
     *
     * Because this is using `static` instead
of `self`
     * it will use the property of the class
that was invoked when instantiating the object.
     * This is very helpful for extending the
class but it still doesn't have access to the
object.
     *
     * @returns string
     */
    static public function get_prefix() {
        return static::$prefix;
    }
}


class Doctor extends Person {
    /**
     * Prefix used to identify the Person.
```

```php
         *
         * @param string
         */
    static $prefix = 'Dr. ';
}


class Man extends Person {
    /**
         * Prefix used to identify the Person.
         *
         * @param string
         */
    static $prefix = 'Mr. ';
}


class Unmarried_Woman extends Person {
    /**
         * Prefix used to identify the Person.
         *
         * @param string
         */
    static $prefix = 'Miss ';
}


class Married_Woman extends Person {
    /**
         * Prefix used to identify the Person.
         *
         * @param string
         */
    static $prefix = 'Mrs. ';
}
```

I extended this a few times to show how it works. Now you can generate objects that are people, doctors, men, and married or unmarried women (which matters with the prefix used in English and a few other languages).

There are two different ways that I accessed the static methods and properties. Both use ":::" to indicate it is using a static property or method instead of "->", which would be used to access an object property or method.

The "static::" expression is a fun little trick that references the invoked class, so "echo Doctor::get_prefix();" will output "Dr. " instead of "". It saves having to create a "get_prefix()" method in every single class.

To be honest, it would probably be better to make this a public function, but if there were an instance where I needed access to "get_prefix()" without the full object, then this is the simplest way to do that.

It's also important to know what "static" means when looking at the Sanitize class.

THE SANITIZER CLASS

Genesis_Settings_Sanitizer came in Genesis 1.7 and was the second class to be added to Genesis. It has proven to be very helpful for Genesis and also for third party plugins and themes that add options.

There are several ways to interact with the class, but the main method is to use the "genesis_add_option_filter" function (also found in this file) to add an option that will be filtered. It's very easy to do.

```
add_action( 'genesis_settings_sanitizer_init',
'child_register_social_sanitization_filters' );
/**
 * Register additional Sensitization options.
 */
```

```
function
child_register_social_sanitization_filters() {
        // These are URLs so should be
sanitized as URLs.
        genesis_add_option_filter(
                'url',
                GENESIS_SETTINGS_FIELD,
                array(
                        'twitter_url',
                        'facebook_url',
                )
        );

        // This is a string that will never
have HTML so should be sanitized with no HTML
        genesis_add_option_filter(
                'no_html',
                GENESIS_SETTINGS_FIELD,
                array(
                        'twitter_handle',
                )
        );
}
```

As you see, you don't need to know OOP in order to use this. There is a convenient function that registered all the settings, and then the class will handle the rest of the work. The code should be run on the "genesis_settings_sanitizer_init" hook because it ensures the functions are available and also that the save actions have not already completed. Using this method ensures that data being saved is safe when it hits the database.

There are several methods available:

- one_zero

- no_html

- absint

- safe_html

- requires_unfiltered_html

- unfiltered_or_safe_html

- url

- email_address

It is also possible to use the "genesis_available_sanitizer_filters" filter to alter these values or register new sanitization functions.

Most of the methods are public but the really cool thing is you do not need to instantiate a new instance of the object because of the static "$instance" property.

If you check out the the code in the "genesis_add_option_filter" function, you will find that the "add_filter" method is accessed via the "$instance" like this:

```
return
Genesis_Settings_Sanitizer::$instance->add_filte
r( $filter, $option, $suboption );
```

This means all the methods can also be accessed in the same way.

So if you are saving post meta (which wouldn't normally use this class), you can pass your content through the sanitize methods.

I do something like this:

```
class Child_Save_Post {

    /**
     * Registers the save post callback.
     */
```

```php
    public function __construct() {
        add_action( 'save_post', array( $this,
'save_post' ) );
    }

    /**
     * Save post callback saves the post meta
     */
    public function save_post( $post_id ) {
        // Do some conditional checks to verify
the post type, nonce, post status, and anything
else that matters for this action.
        $sanitize = array(
            'no_html' => array(
                'option_1',
                'option_2',
            ),
            'one_zero' => array(
                'option_3',
            ),
        );

        foreach ( $sanitize as $method =>
$options ) {
            foreach ( $options as $option ) {
                $value = isset( $_GET[ $option
] ) ? $_GET[ $option ] : '';
                update_post_meta( $post_id,
$option,
Genesis_Settings_Sanitizer::$instance->$method(
$value ) );
            }
        }
    }
```

```
}
new Child_Save_Post();
```

This really needs a bit of work to improve security by adding the nonce, and it might need to account for potentially some other ways of doing the sanitization. However, I think the basic idea is there. It is possible to use the Sanitize class via the static "$instance" for any data that should be sanitized, which is all data.

THE SCRIPT LOADER CLASS

In reviewing the classes so far, you've learned more about OOP. You've learned about the difference between classes and objects, how to limit access to properties and methods, and how to access certain properties and methods without creating a new object. It's been a lot to take in, and I'm glad to reach a class that is much more accessible.

In fact, you don't need to know anything about the class in order to use it.

I was fortunate to be able to contribute to this class. I realized that accessing certain Genesis scripts meant adding them as new scripts in each plugin, which is far from efficient. I proposed that Genesis should register all the scripts then enqueue as needed. Previously it was doing a good job of enqueueing as needed, but the scripts weren't registered. So, they were only available as needed.

Now child themes and plugins can require the Genesis scripts when enqueueing their own scripts, which makes it much easier to access and use the Genesis scripts.

GENESIS_SCRIPT_LOADER

This is a very straight forward class. The object is instantiated in the lib/scripts/load-scripts.php file and the "add_hooks" method is called right after creating the object.

The "add_hooks" method adds four actions, two each on "wp_enqueue_scripts" and "admin_enqueue_scripts".

The first two are added with a priority of 0, and they register all the Genesis scripts. This ensures that those scripts will be available to any plugin or child theme so long as they use a priority of 1 or greater.

The last two load with the default priority of 10 and will enqueue the scripts that are needed for a given page load.

They also use the "wp_localize_script" function in order to add internationalized strings that are output via the scripts.

That is all there is to the class. You don't need to know anything about objects for most of the ways you might take advantage of this. There is one caveat to this, but we will talk about that in the next chapter.

USING GENESIS SCRIPTS

The real trick here is how you can use Genesis scripts.

So let's say you are creating a WordPress admin page for your theme or plugin. Being a very conscientious developer, you know you shouldn't load your admin scripts on every page.

You use some conditional logic to make sure your "wp_enqueue_script" function only loads on the intended screen. You are working well ahead of the curve, and I commend you.

Only, you realize you need the "genesis_admin_js" script on your page. With the way this is done now, it is super easy.

```
wp_register_script( 'child_admin_js',
URL_TO_JS_DIRECTORY . "/child-admin.js", array(
'jquery', 'genesis_admin_js' ), '0.0.1', true );
```

All you have to do is add "genesis_admin_js" as a required JS
handled just like "jquery", and it will make sure that your script is
loaded **after** the Genesis admin script. It is literally that easy, and
that is all you need to know about this file (for now).

WHAT'S NEXT?

So now you understand how the sanitize and script loader classes
work and you understand what the static keyword does.

There's one last thing to understand about classes.

In the next chapter, we will look at how actions and filters are
affected by OOP.

CHAPTER 16.

GENESIS ACTIONS AND FILTERS IN CLASSES EXPLAINED

In this section of the book we've explored classes in Genesis.

So far you have learned about action and filter callbacks and a lot about classes, but there is one last thing to understand: How do action and filter callbacks work with classes?

That is going to be the topic of this final chapter on classes.

ADD_ACTION

If you look carefully at the classes from the previous chapters, you can see some actions and filters being used with the classes.

```
add_action( 'wp_enqueue_scripts',    array(
$this, 'register_front_scripts' ), 0 );
add_filter( 'sanitize_option_' . $option,
array( $this, 'sanitize' ), 10, 2 );
```

When working with a class, the callback is formed using an array. The first item in the array is the class or object and the second item is the method.

There was something important in that description. Did you

notice the "or"? That is right, the callback can use a class **or** object.

If you remember the class is the code, and the object is the instantiated class.

When using the class, the method must be static. This is very important and is a mistake developers often make.

```
class Has_Callback {
    function callback() {
    }
}
add_action( 'hook', array( 'Has_Callback',
'callback' );
```

That will generate an error because the callback method isn't static.

```
class Has_Callback {
    static function callback() {
    }
}
add_action( 'hook', array( 'Has_Callback',
'callback' );
```

That will work just fine, but remember the object will not be available in the static method. If the object is needed, it will need to be accessed by instantiating it since "$this" will return an error.

It is possible to instantiate the object and add that to the action.

```
class Has_Callback {
    function callback() {
    }
}
```

```
$object = new Has_Callback();
add_action( 'hook', array( $object, 'callback'
);
```

That will work, and when you do that "$this" is available inside the callback. This is is a great way to do it, but there are drawbacks. It will become much more evident when we get to the information about removing the actions and filters.

Finally, it is possible to have a function that returns the object or to use the static property that holds the object.

If you remember from the Sanitize class, the "$instance" property is static and holds the object after "admin_init" has been run. This means it would be possible to use the methods in a filter like:

```
add_filter( 'filter', array(
Genesis_Settings_Sanitizer::$instance,
'sanitize' ), 10, 2 );
```

Alternately, if you look at the lib/js/load-scripts.php file, you will find the "genesis_scripts" function:

```
function genesis_scripts() {

        static $_genesis_scripts = null;

        if ( null === $_genesis_scripts ) {

                require_once( PARENT_DIR .
'/lib/classes/class-genesis-script-loader.php'
);
                $_genesis_scripts = new
Genesis_Script_Loader();
                $_genesis_scripts->add_hooks();
```

```
        }

        return $_genesis_scripts;

}
```

This uses a static variable to instantiate the "Genesis_Script_Loader" object and returns it. This ensures one instance of the class when using this function to get the object. This will be very important in the remove action section. A function like this can be used to easily add actions. This could be useful if you ever wanted to have the front end scripts registered for the dashboard like this:

```
add_action( 'admin_enqueue_scripts', array(
genesis_scripts(), 'register_front_scripts' ),
0 );
```

Those are the methods for adding actions and filters with a class. There are several benefits but also some limitations.

As I already noted, depending on the method you use, you must have a static method and will not have access to the object. There are also potential disadvantages when it comes to removing actions and filters.

REMOVE_ACTION

If you remember back to the chapters on actions and filters, the remove action or filter must exactly match the add action or filter. The filter, callback, priority, and accepted number of arguments have to be exactly the same.

This is simple enough when the add action or filter uses the class.

```
add_action( 'hook', array( 'Has_Callback',
'callback' );
```

This is removed like:

```
remove_action( 'hook', array( 'Has_Callback',
'callback' );
```

However, when the code uses the object, you need the same object in order to remove it. Often actions and filters are added within the class using "$this".

For example, in the Script Loader class it uses code like this:

```
add_action( 'wp_enqueue_scripts',    array(
$this, 'enqueue_front_scripts' ) );
```

You cannot use "$this" unless you are in the same object.

```
remove_action( 'wp_enqueue_scripts',    array(
$this, 'enqueue_front_scripts' ) );
```

Most of the time that will not work.

You also can't use the class.

```
remove_action( 'wp_enqueue_scripts',    array(
'Genesis_Script_Loader',
'enqueue_front_scripts' ) );
```

Since the action was added with the object, this doesn't match.

Now you might think, "Hey, I'll get an object, and then I can remove it."

```
$script_loader = new Genesis_Script_Loader ();
remove_action( 'wp_enqueue_scripts',    array(
$script_loader, 'enqueue_front_scripts' ) );
```

That will not work either because "$script_load" is a **new** and **different** object. That means it will not exactly match.

This is very frustrating and has caused me a lot of grief, but there are ways to get the object. It won't work everywhere, but using what we've learned about the Genesis classes so far, it is possible to discover how to get some of the objects.

The Script Loader, as I've mentioned, has a function that will set the object to a static variable that it will return. The action can be removed using that function.

```
remove_action( 'wp_enqueue_scripts',    array(
genesis_scripts(), 'enqueue_front_scripts' ) );
```

This works because it is the exact same object, so it matches the "$this" used when adding the action.

For the Sanitize class, there is a static "$instance" variable that is available in the class.

```
add_filter( 'sanitize_option_my_option', array(
Genesis_Settings_Sanitizer::$instance,
'sanitize' ), 10, 2 );
```

That is the biggest drawback to using the object in an action/ filter. However, once you can learn to work with this, then it becomes second nature to find how to work with it. Hopefully you'll also feel comfortable using it to make your code easy to interact with, just like these Genesis classes.

WHAT'S NEXT?

The class section is coming to a close. The next section covers the Genesis admin, which also includes some classes. So what you've learned about classes will be a good foundation for understanding how the admin works.

The good news is the hard part is over. Conquering actions, filters, and classes is the most difficult part of working with Genesis. You are now prepared to reach the summit and stand proud as one of the elite.

CHAPTER 17.

GENESIS ADMIN OVERVIEW EXPLAINED

In this part of the book, we're going to explore the Admin area of Genesis.

In this first chapter, I will focus on a general overview of the Admin files in Genesis.

In the subsequent chapters, we'll dive into individual Admin files and functions. I recommend opening the Genesis folder and looking at the files as I describe them. This will help you become more familiar with them so you can reference them later.

It is very important to start to understand how the files are arranged and to take advantage of the internal documentation. The admin of Genesis tends to update much more frequently and with much greater difference than the front end part of the site.

When I originally wrote the Genesis Explained series, the admin was controlled via static functions; and the way a developer interacted with it was very different from how it is done with the modern, OOP methods used today.

Even now there is a big push in Genesis to move the theme settings into the WordPress customizer. There are many settings that benefit significantly from this because those settings affect the appearance of the site, and changes can be seen in real time.

As of WordPress 4.9, they can even be saved as draft and scheduled.

GENESIS ADMIN FILES

Open the genesis/lib/admin folder, and this is what you should see

- /images
- admin-functions.php
- cpt-archive-settings.php
- customizer.php
- import-export.php
- inpost-metaboxes.php
- menu.php
- seo-settings.php
- term-meta.php
- theme-settings.php
- use-child-theme.php
- user-meta.php
- whats-new.php

The first item is an images folder and includes the images used in the dashboard. Then it moves on to some files. Here is a brief overview of them. Remember, I will go into more detail of each file in the following chapters, unless noted.

admin-functions.php

This has one function, but it is a helpful function. "genesis_meta_boxes()" returns a single instance of the "Genesis_Admin_Meta_Boxes" class. This allows developers to get and interact with a single object when using the metabox class. This will come up in later chapters.

cpt-archive-settings.php

This has the "Genesis_Admin_CPT_Archive_Settings" class. It will generate multiple archive pages and make them subpages of the Custom Post Type that supports the genesis-cpt-archive. For the most part, you do not directly interact with this object, but there are some helpful filters for modifying the archive pages. This class also serves as a great example of an advanced means of generating dynamic admin pages with the Genesis admin classes.

customizer.php

This file has two classes: "Genesis_Customizer_Base" and "Genesis_Customizer". The former is an abstract class that can be used to interact with the WordPress customizer. The later extends the abstract class to add Genesis options to the customizer. This not only adds options to the customizer, but demonstrates how the "Genesis_Customizer_Base" can be used.

import-export.php

This file enables and creates the import export functionality within Genesis. With this you can copy Genesis settings to another site. It will not copy over widgets and their settings, but anything in the registered settings field can be exported.

This is done via the "Genesis_Admin_Import_Export" class. Originally there were static functions, but with updates it was moved to OOP.

inpost-metaboxes.php

This file creates the meta boxes for the posts, pages, and other post types that might be using them.

I want to define "meta boxes" since the term is used several times, but it isn't necessarily understood. The post "meta" is information that is attached to a post. This is typically a custom field, but there is actually a good deal of meta information. For the sake of this, we'll just say "custom fields". For more information, you can read up on this over at the WP Codex. Start with the Post Meta Examples, and drill down to other details. A meta box is an extra box for adding meta information to the post or page. The term meta and user meta work the same, with respect to terms and user details.

The default meta boxes include the SEO settings, Scripts, and Layout Options.

Unlike many other admin files, this is a series of static functions. This means it is still a nice oasis in the class heavy admin files.

menu.php

This file creates the actual "Genesis" menu and the tabs under it. The functions here are still simple, static functions with traditional WordPress admin actions, but this file received a significant makeover in Genesis 1.8 when the admin classes were introduced. Now the functions instantiate and interact with the admin objects to generate the menu items and the pages they link to.

seo-settings.php

This file creates the SEO settings page, which is accessed under Genesis > SEO Settings.

term-meta.php

This file creates the extra meta boxes for terms. Terms is a catch all for categories, tags, and other taxonomies that might be added.

This file has gone through several revisions. The first was when the "genesis_meta_boxes()" function and related class was added. More recently it was updated to deal with changes in WordPress support for term meta. Previously the term data was saved in an option table and Genesis had to do a fair bit of heavy lifting to make it all work. After WordPress added official support for term meta, this file and other functionality in Genesis was modified to take advantage of that.

However, there were some growing pains because failing to take the traditional upgrade path could cause term data to be lost. The folks behind Genesis worked very hard to make sure that didn't happen and added scripts that updated the database and put term data into the WordPress term meta. They also added a fallback to account for people who may have taken the upgrade path differently. This actually caused big issues with site load times, so the fallback had to be removed. Fortunately by then most users had completed the upgrade path and didn't lose data, or they followed the planned upgrade path and kept their data.

Either way, this is a great example of all the hard work and thought that goes into preparing for a WordPress update.

theme-settings.php

This file creates the main Genesis theme settings and sets up the hook for adding additional meta boxes to the theme settings. The hook works differently than the other Genesis Hooks since it is built form WordPress core functionality.

The "Genesis_Admin_Settings" does the work and is another good example of how to use the Genesis Admin Classes to add an admin page to the site.

use-child-theme.php

One issue that comes up regularly is people using the Genesis theme instead of a Genesis child theme. There are several drawbacks to this. Many times people think, "I'm not going to modify the theme, so why not use the Genesis theme?"

Aside from losing any edits to the theme with updates, using the Genesis theme means a big potential to have the design of the site changed. Most updates include a redesign of the Genesis core appearance and an accompanying Genesis Sample Child Theme. When the base theme is the desired look, then that sample theme can be used with no downside.

This file adds a notice that Genesis is active without a child theme and something should be done about it.

One nice thing in the file is the use of the Genesis Views. This is a way to move HTML out of the core files to simplify maintenance and make the files easier to read.

user-meta.php

This file creates and loads the extra meta boxes in the user profile pages.

The file uses static functions but takes advantage of the "genesis_meta_boxes()" object to build output.

whats-new.php

This last file creates the "What's New" page. This includes a view page for maintainability and to make the file much easier to read and understand.

WHAT'S NEXT?

Again, I encourage you to read through the files. They are already documented to explain the functions and you will have a good head start for the next chapter.

After you have read through the files to see how the Genesis admin classes are being used in Genesis, you will have a better idea of how the Admin classes work, which is really convenient because the next subject is the Admin classes.

CHAPTER 18.

GENESIS ADMIN CLASS EXPLAINED

Genesis 1.8 introduced a whole new admin system. When I first started writing about the admin side of Genesis, the system was getting a complete overhaul. It was fascinating to watch the new system be created from the first discussion through to the 1.8 implementation.

When it was all said and done, I was able to write about how to work with the new admin system. I also created a builder class to make it even easier to implement with standard markup. The code for the builder class is in GitHub and available via this URL: http://nickc.co/admin-builder.

Even without the builder class, it is pretty simple to work with the new Genesis Admin Classes. If you look at the cpt-archive-settings.php, seo-settings.php, or theme-settings.php files, you will see some examples of how the classes work.

If you open the genesis/lib/classes/admin.php file, you will see all the code that forms the basis for the Genesis Admin OOP system. There are four abstract classes that make up the abstraction layer.

This brings up a big question for people unfamiliar with OOP.

WHAT IS ABSTRACTION?

In the classes section I explained a fair bit about classes and objects. Keywords like public, protected, private, and static were all explained. Abstract is another concept that lives at the class level.

Classes are very powerful because they can extend other classes, so the objects inherit the parent class methods and properties. We talked about this concept with the Person class and child classes like Doctor. The big advantage is the code can be DRY.

DRY EXPLAINED

DRY means "Don't Repeat Yourself". The idea is that if you have the same code more than once, it should become a function, class, or other repeatable content. Code that is DRY is easier to use, understand, and maintain. For example, a function like, "genesis_code" does one very simple, little job. It wraps the provided string in HTML code tags.

This is easy to use because the function can be dropped in anywhere.

It is easy to understand because the function is well documented, the function name strongly hints at the purpose, and it results in clean, readable code compared to using other methods to add the code tags manually.

Finally, it is maintainable. If, for some reason, WordPress core changed their style to target an element with `class="wp-code"` instead of the plain code tag, it would mean one simple update in one function could fix all instances using that function. Without a function like this, the code would have to be updated in multiple files and there is a good chance that the code would be missed.

So DRY code is good code.

Well, it doesn't always, but that is a big part of what it is supposed to do. An abstract class doesn't work on its own. It will have methods that are flagged as "abstract", and if you try to build an object from that class, it will fail.

Think of a class like a skeleton. When you instantiate the class, it becomes an object which lets you start manipulating the skeleton. You might change a property that makes the bones longer, or you might use a method that causes the leg to raise. Lot's of cool things happen when interacting with the object, but if the skeleton is an abstract class, it would just be a pile of bones, not a workable object. The abstract methods are kind of like having a sign on the skeleton that says, "insert spine here".

The great thing about the abstract class is a lot of important parts are available. It can be extended, and the missing parts can be added.

In our skeleton example, we might have an abstract method for the spine, hips, and skull. Then the leg, ribs, and arms methods could be replaced as needed by the child class. By filling in the blanks, we get bipedal and quadrupedal skeletons without having to define every single bone, just the properties and methods that are different. Some animals have more or less bones and some have different configurations of bones, but among vertebrates there are a lot of commonalities.

In fact, if we define the base "Vertebrate_Skeleton" class first with the parts that all vertebrates have like a spine, skull, and the definition of a bone, then we can make additional abstract classes for fish, birds, lizards, snakes, mammals, quadrupeds, bipeds, and eventually humans. Each abstract class can become a final class that defines the exact nature of the animal's skeleton.

This all works together so that the code doesn't have to be repeated, and only the differences are defined at each level.

GENESIS ABSTRACT ADMIN CLASSES

So now that you have an idea about the abstract concept, let's consider the Genesis classes. As I said, there are 4 total classes:

- Genesis_Admin
- Genesis_Admin_Form
- Genesis_Admin_Boxes
- Genesis_Admin_Basic

GENESIS_ADMIN

This is the base abstract class. The other three classes extend this class. In general, this class is not really intended to be extended by a final class directly. It can be, but it requires a bit more work. Instead, it is supposed to be extended by another class, which will be extended to create the admin page output.

There are:

- 12 public methods
- 6 protected methods
- 6 public properties
- 2 protected properties
- 2 abstract methods

The abstract methods **must** be extended by another class, and they must be public, since the methods in this class are public.

THE "CREATE()" METHOD

The "create()" method is the backbone (to steal from the analogy I used about abstraction) of the entire Genesis Admin system. This method is typically called inside another method in the final class in order to create the admin page.

create($page_id = ", array $menu_ops = array(), array $page_ops = array(), $settings_field = ", array $default_settings = array())

This method takes five possible arguments. Those arguments define where the page is added in the menu and how it is described.

For example, this is the "_construct()" function in the "Genesis_Admin_Settings" class. It is responsible for creating the Genesis menu item and the Genesis Theme Settings page.

```
/**
         * Create an admin menu item and
settings page.
         *
         * @since 1.8.0
         */
        public function __construct() {

                $page_id = 'genesis';

                $menu_ops = apply_filters(
'genesis_theme_settings_menu_ops',
                        array(
                                'main_menu' =>
array(
                                        'sep'
=> array(

'sep_position'   => '58.995',

'sep_capability' => 'edit_theme_options',
```

```php
                                          ),

'page_title' => 'Theme Settings',

'menu_title' => 'Genesis',

'capability' => 'edit_theme_options',

'icon_url'   => GENESIS_ADMIN_IMAGES_URL .
'/genesis-menu.png',

'position'   => '58.996',
                                          ),
                                          'first_submenu'
=> array( // Do not use without 'main_menu'.

'page_title' => __( 'Theme Settings', 'genesis'
),

'menu_title' => __( 'Theme Settings', 'genesis'
),

'capability' => 'edit_theme_options',
                                          ),
                        )
                    );

                $page_ops = apply_filters(

'genesis_theme_settings_page_ops',
                        array(

'save_button_text'  => __( 'Save Changes',
'genesis' ),
```

```php
'reset_button_text' => __( 'Reset Settings',
'genesis' ),

'saved_notice_text' => __( 'Settings saved.',
'genesis' ),

'reset_notice_text' => __( 'Settings reset.',
'genesis' ),

'error_notice_text' => __( 'Error saving
settings.', 'genesis' ),
                )
        );

            $settings_field =
GENESIS_SETTINGS_FIELD;

            $default_settings =
apply_filters(

'genesis_theme_settings_defaults',
                    array(

'update'                    => 1,

'update_email'              => 0,

'update_email_address'      => '',

'blog_title'                => 'text',

'style_selection'           => '',

'site_layout'               =>
genesis_get_default_layout(),
```

```
'superfish'                     => 0,

'nav_extras'                    => '',

'nav_extras_twitter_id'         => '',

'nav_extras_twitter_text'       => __( 'Follow me
on Twitter', 'genesis' ),

'feed_uri'                      => '',

'redirect_feed'                 => 0,

'comments_feed_uri'             => '',

'redirect_comments_feed'        => 0,

'comments_pages'                => 0,

'comments_posts'                => 1,

'trackbacks_pages'              => 0,

'trackbacks_posts'              => 1,

'breadcrumb_home'               => 0,

'breadcrumb_front_page'         => 0,

'breadcrumb_posts_page'         => 0,

'breadcrumb_single'             => 0,

'breadcrumb_page'               => 0,
```

```
'breadcrumb_archive'          => 0,

'breadcrumb_404'              => 0,

'breadcrumb_attachment'       => 0,

'content_archive'             => 'full',

'content_archive_thumbnail' => 0,

'image_size'                  => '',

'image_alignment'             => 'alignleft',

'posts_nav'                   => 'numeric',

'blog_cat'                    => '',

'blog_cat_exclude'            => '',

'blog_cat_num'                => 10,

'header_scripts'              => '',

'footer_scripts'              => '',

'theme_version'               =>
PARENT_THEME_VERSION,

'db_version'                  =>
PARENT_DB_VERSION,

'first_version'               =>
genesis_first_version(),
```

```
                    )
            );

            $this->create( $page_id,
$menu_ops, $page_ops, $settings_field,
$default_settings );

            add_action(
'genesis_settings_sanitizer_init', array(
$this, 'sanitizer_filters' ) );


        }
```

I should mention that the "_construct()" function is a special function that is called when an object is created. In this case, the code "new Genesis_Admin_Settings();" would run that function automatically.

"page_id" is set as "genesis". This makes the page use that for the page hook and some filters that are run. It is part of the menu and admin page.

"$menu_ops" has several arguments. It is set as a "main_menu" and will have a separator added to the menu. This position is just before the Genesis menu position, so if you log into your dashboard you will notice that there is a small break before the Genesis menu.

The "page_title" and "menu_title" are fairly self explanatory. The first is for the admin page and the second is for the menu title in the left admin menu.

There is also a "first_submenu" item further down the list that sets the submenu page that appears on the flyout when hovering on the item, or at the top of the submenu when on the Genesis settings pages.

`capability` uses the WordPress capabilities to define who has access to the page and who can see the page in the menu. In this case only users with the ability to edit theme options (admins by default) can see the menu item or access the settings page.

The final items are for "icon_url" and "position". The Icon URL points to the genesis-menu.png file, and the position is set to roughly halfway down the menu (depending on how many menu items there are).

`$page_ops` is a bit more simple. The accepted keys set the save button, reset button, saved notice, reset notice, and error notice texts.

Finally, there is the "$settings_field" and "$default_settings" values. The first sets the page to register the "GENESIS_SETTINGS_FIELD" setting field, and the second registers the default settings. These will be used when initially setting up the options and if the reset button is used. It has a helpful filter for plugins and themes that add additional metaboxes with settings to the Genesis Theme Settings page.

As you can see, this functions sets up and does a lot. It can take several different kinds of input, like instead of "main_menu" it could be a "submenu".

In the sea-settings.php file, the menu ops are much simpler and show how the "submenu" works.

```
$menu_ops = array(
        'submenu' => array(
                'parent_slug'
=> 'genesis',
                'page_title'
=> __( 'Genesis - SEO Settings', 'genesis' ),
                'menu_title'
=> __( 'SEO Settings', 'genesis' ),
```

```
                                )  ,
            )  ;
```

This requires a "parent_slug" in addition to the "page_title" and "menu_title" that were seen previously. As you can see in this example, the menu item it is added to is "genesis", which was the "$page_id" used to create the Genesis Theme Settings page.

OTHER METHODS

Most of the other methods support the create method in some way. They register the menu item and settings. They handle basic save functionality. They even prepare help screens. Most of the items aren't used directly though.

settings_init()

This is the first of two abstract methods. It is intended to initialize the settings. The other three abstract classes all extend this method. In general, that is where the magic happens, and it doesn't need to be extended again.

admin()

This is the other abstract method. "Genesis_Admin_Forms" and "Genesis_Admin_Boxes" both extend this method so it doesn't have to be extended again. If the "Genesis_Admin_Basic" class is used, it must be extended.

This method is used as the callback for the "admin_menu_page" function, so it creates the admin page output. In most cases, the Forms and Boxes methods will be the best place to start. However, if there is need for a custom output that doesn't use the Forms or Boxes HTML, then the Basic class is where you will start.

get_field_name($name)

This is a helper function that generates the "[{$setting_field}]{$name}" output. This helps to standardize the output and makes it easy to update. Use it with inputs and select boxes to automatically get the correct name attribute.

To automatically echo the attribute, use the "field_name($name)" method.

get_field_id($id)

This is exactly like the "get_field_name" method right now, but it may change at some point to generate a valid output for the id attribute. Use this or the "field_id($id)" method to output the id attribute of select and input fields. This can also be used on labels to create the for attribute.

get_field_value($key)

This gets the value from the settings field for the provided key. The "$key" should match the "$name" value for the "get_field_name" method. It can but doesn't need to match the "$id" argument for the "get_field_id" method. "field_value($key)" will echo the value instead of return it.

WHAT'S NEXT?

Now that you understand the base Genesis_Admin class and how abstraction works, it is time to look at the three classes that you will be extending to access the admin class.

The Genesis_Admin_Form, Genesis_Admin_Boxes, and Genesis_Admin_Basic classes are the next layer of the foundation that Genesis admin pages are built with.

CHAPTER 19.

GENESIS ADMIN BOXES, FORM AND BASIC CLASSES EXPLAINED

Welcome to the final chapter of Gensis Explained.

So far you have learned about actions, filters, functions, and most of the Genesis classes as well as helpful information about how classes work.

This last section deals with the Genesis admin classes for boxes, forms, and the basic class. These all extend the Genesis_Admin class to provide additional features. The Genesis_Admin_Form does a simple form without metaboxes, Genesis_Admin_Boxes are interred to work with metaboxes, and Genesis_Admin_Basic starts with a completely blank slate. The latter is best used for informational pages without settings.

GENESIS_ADMIN_FORM

This extends the "Genesis_Admin" class and the "settings_init" and "admin" methods. This means you will not need to extend those methods. It adds a new abstract method, `form()`, that will need to be extended though.

It also makes use of the genesis-admin-form page view to handle the HTML output of the page. As I mentioned before, the views make it easier to read the code because there isn't a big block of

HTML in the middle of the output. It is also easier to maintain because the HTML is in one convenient place. However, it does mean you need to open that file to see how this is output. It is in genesis/inc/views/pages/genesis-admin-form.php.

As you can see, it generates a page with a wrap, title, and form HTML. Buttons are automatically output at the bottom of the form. There is a "do_action" that handles getting content into the form HTML.

The "settings_init" method automatically adds the correct action so that the "form" method will load on the page.

To use this you have to extend the "form" method when you extend this class. Here is a super simple example.

```
/**
 * Registers a new admin page, providing
content and corresponding menu item for the
Child Theme Settings page.
 *
 * Although this class was added in 1.8.0, some
of the methods were originally standalone
functions added in previous
 * versions of Genesis.
 *
 * @package Genesis\Admin
 *
 * @since 1.8.0
 */
class Child_Settings extends Genesis_Admin_Form
{

        /**
         * Create an admin menu item and
settings page.
```

```php
         *
         * @since 1.8.0
         */
        public function __construct() {

                $page_id = 'child-settings';

                $menu_ops = array(
                        'submenu' => array(
                                'parent_slug'
=> 'genesis',
                                'page_title'
=> __( 'Child Settings', 'child' ),
                                'menu_title'
=> __( 'Child Settings', 'child' ),
                        ),
                );

                $page_ops = array(
                        'save_button_text'  =>
__( 'Save Changes', 'child' ),
                        'reset_button_text' =>
__( 'Reset Settings', 'child' ),
                        'saved_notice_text' =>
__( 'Settings saved.', 'child' ),
                        'reset_notice_text' =>
__( 'Settings reset.', 'child' ),
                        'error_notice_text' =>
__( 'Error saving settings.', 'child' ),
                );

                $settings_field =
'child-theme-settings';

                $default_settings = array(
```

```php
                    'text_field'   => '',
                    'checkbox'     => '',
                    'select_field' => '',
            );

            $this->create( $page_id,
$menu_ops, $page_ops, $settings_field,
$default_settings );

            add_action(
'genesis_settings_sanitizer_init', array(
$this, 'sanitizer_filters' ) );

        }

        /**
         * Register each of the settings with a
sanitization filter type.
         *
         * @since 1.7.0
         *
         * @see
\Genesis_Settings_Sanitizer::add_filter() Add
sanitization filters to options.
         */
        public function sanitizer_filters() {

                genesis_add_option_filter(
                        'one_zero',
                        $this->settings_field,
                        array(
                                'checkbox',
                        )
                );
```

```php
                genesis_add_option_filter(
                        'no_html',
                        $this->settings_field,
                        array(
                                'text_field',
                                'select_field',
                        )
                );

        }


        /**
         * Output Form Fields on page.
         *
         * @since 1.0.0
         */
        public function form() {
<table class="form-table">
<tbody>
<tr valign="top">
<th scope="row">
    <label for="<?php $this->field_id(
'text_field' ); ?>">
        <?php _e( 'Text Field Label,
'my-domain' ); ?>
    </label>
 </th>
<td>
    <input
        name="<?php $this->field_name(
'text_field' ); ?>"
        type="text"
        id="<?php $this->field_id( 'text_field'
); ?>"
```

```
        value="<?php $this->field_value(
'text_field' ); ?>"
        class="regular-text"
    />
</td>
</tr>
<tr valign="top">
<th scope="row">
    <label for="<?php $this->field_id(
'checkbox' ); >">
        <?php _e( 'Label for checkbox',
'my-domain' ); ?>
    </label>
</th>
<td>
    <input
        name="<?php $this->field_name(
'checkbox' ); ?>"
        type="checkbox"
        id="<?php $this->field_id( 'checkbox'
); ?>"
        value="1"
        <?php checked( 1,
$this->get_field_value( 'checkbox' ), true ); ?>
    />
</td>
</tr>
<tr valign="top">
<th scope="row">
    <label for="<?php $this->field_id(
'select_field' ); ?>">
        <?php _e( 'Label for select box',
'my-domain' ); ?>
    </label>
</th>
```

```
<td>
    <select
        name="<?php $this->field_name(
'select_field' ); ?>"
        type="checkbox"
        id="<?php $this->field_id(
'select_field' ); ?>"
    >
        <option value="one" <?php selected(
'one', $this->get_field_value( 'select_field'
), true ); ?>>
        <option value="two" <?php selected(
'two', $this->get_field_value( 'select_field'
), true ); ?>>
    </select>
</td>
</tr>
</tbody>
</table>
?>
<?php } }
```

So you can see this registered a child page of the Genesis theme settings page. It is using the "Genesis_Admin_Form" class in order to create the form HTML output. The sanitizer filter is being used to ensure when the settings are saved. They are sanitized before sending to the database.

The "form" method is extended and uses pretty standard form HTML. The nonce, form wrapper, and buttons are all taken care of automatically so it only needs the inner form HTML.

GENESIS_ADMIN_BOXES

Similar to the "Genesis_Admin_Form" class, the "admin" and "settings_init" methods are both extended by this class. It also adds new abstraction via the "metaboxes" method. Also, like the Form class, this uses the genesis-admin-boxes view to set the base HTML.

If you open genesis/lib/views/genesis-admin-boxes.php file, you will see a wrap, title, and form not unlike the form view. There is a "do_action" for the page boxes and some javascript that makes it possible to toggle the metaboxes open and closed.

The settings init adds the "do_metaboxes" method to the page "do_action" and sets up the "metaboxes" method to add metaboxes to the page.

Let's look at the SEO settings to see how the "metaboxes" method works:

```
/**
 * Register meta boxes on the SEO
Settings page.
 *
 * @since 1.0.0
 */
public function metaboxes() {

        $this->add_meta_box(
'genesis-seo-settings-sitewide', __( 'Site-wide
Settings', 'genesis' ) );
        $this->add_meta_box(
'genesis-seo-settings-homepage', __( 'Homepage
Settings', 'genesis' ) );
        $this->add_meta_box(
'genesis-seo-settings-dochead', __( 'Document
Head Settings', 'genesis' ) );
        $this->add_meta_box(
'genesis-seo-settings-robots', __( 'Robots Meta
Settings', 'genesis' ) );
```

```
        }
```

As you can see, this calls a simple method that adds the meta boxes. When you look at the "add_meta_box" method, you will see that it adds all the metaboxes to the same callback.

```
add_meta_box( $handle, $title, array( $this,
'do_meta_box' ), $this->pagehook, 'main',
$priority );
```

This works well because Genesis is using views to control the output.

```
            $view = $this->views_base .
'/meta-boxes/' . $meta_box['id'] . '.php';
            if ( is_file( $view ) ) {
                    include( $view );
            }
```

You can do something very similar in the child theme or plugin.

You need to add this to the `_construct()` function for your child theme:

```
$this->views_base = get_stylesheet_directory() .
'/lib/views/';
```

If you are using a plugin, then this is a good approach:

First, create a constant in the main plugin file like:

```
define(                    'MY_GENESIS_PLUGIN_DIR',
plugin_dir_path( __FILE__ ) );
```

Then you can register your views_base like:

```php
$this->views_base   =   MY_GENESIS_PLUGIN_DIR   .
'/lib/views/';
```

In both cases, you can put your view template files in the lib/
views/meta-boxes directory to create your output.

Here is an example view from the SEO settings:

```php
<?php
/**
 * Genesis Framework.
 *
 * WARNING: This file is part of the core
Genesis Framework. DO NOT edit this file under
any circumstances.
 * Please do all modifications in the form of a
child theme.
 *
 * @package StudioPress\Genesis
 * @author  StudioPress
 * @license GPL-2.0+
 * @link    http://my.studiopress.com/themes/
genesis/
 */

?>
<p><span class="description">
   <?php
   $abbrev = sprintf( '<abbr
title="%s">%s</abbr>', __( 'Search engine
optimization', 'genesis' ), __( 'SEO',
'genesis' ) );

   /* translators: Escaped HTML head tag,
abbreviation expansion for SEO. */
   printf( esc_html__( 'By default, WordPress
```

```
places several tags in your document %1$s. Most
of these tags are completely unnecessary, and
provide no %2$s value whatsoever; they just
make your site slower to load. Choose which
tags you would like included in your document
%1$s. If you do not know what something is,
leave it unchecked.', 'genesis' ),
genesis_code( '<head>' ), $abbrev );
    ?>
</span></p>

<table class="form-table">
<tbody>

   <tr valign="top">
      <th scope="row"><?php esc_html_e(
'Relationship Link Tags', 'genesis' ); ?></th>
      <td>
         <p>
            <label for="<?php $this->field_id(
'head_adjacent_posts_rel_link' ); ?>"><input
type="checkbox" name="<?php $this->field_name(
'head_adjacent_posts_rel_link' ); ?>" id="<?php
$this->field_id( 'head_adjacent_posts_rel_link'
); ?>" value="1" <?php checked(
$this->get_field_value(
'head_adjacent_posts_rel_link' ) ); ?> />
            <?php
               /* translators: Meta rel
attribute. */
               printf( esc_html__( 'Adjacent
Posts %s link tags', 'genesis' ), genesis_code(
'rel' ) );
            ?>
            </label>
```

```
        </p>
    </td>
  </tr>

  <tr valign="top">
    <th scope="row"><?php esc_html_e(
'Windows Live Writer', 'genesis' ); ?></th>
    <td>
        <p>
            <label for="<?php $this->field_id(
'head_wlmanifest_link' ); ?>"><input
type="checkbox" name="<?php $this->field_name(
'head_wlwmanifest_link' ); ?>" id="<?php
$this->field_id( 'head_wlmanifest_link' ); ?>"
value="1" <?php checked(
$this->get_field_value( 'head_wlwmanifest_link'
) ); ?> />
            <?php esc_html_e( 'Include Windows
Live Writer Support Tag?', 'genesis' );
?></label>
        </p>
    </td>
  </tr>

  <tr valign="top">
    <th scope="row"><?php esc_html_e(
'Shortlink Tag', 'genesis' ); ?></th>
    <td>
        <p>
            <label for="<?php $this->field_id(
'head_shortlink' ); ?>"><input type="checkbox"
name="<?php $this->field_name( 'head_shortlink'
); ?>" id="<?php $this->field_id(
'head_shortlink' ); ?>" value="1" <?php
checked( $this->get_field_value(
```

```
'head_shortlink' ) ); ?> />
            <?php esc_html_e( 'Include
Shortlink tag?', 'genesis' ); ?></label>
        </p>
        <p>
            <span class="description">
            <?php
                /* translators: Open and close
span tags, abbreviation expansion for SEO. */
                printf( esc_html__( '%sNote:%s
The shortlink tag might have some use for 3rd
party service discoverability, but it has no %s
value whatsoever.', 'genesis' ), '<span
class="genesis-admin-note">', '</span>',
$abbrev );
            ?></span>
        </p>
    </td>
  </tr>

</tbody>
</table>
```

GENESIS_ADMIN_BASIC

The basic class is basic indeed. It extends the `settings_init` method but leaves it blank so it does nothing. It doesn't extend the `admin` class so that must be extended.

This class is very handy for creating informational pages. In fact, if you look at genesis/lib/admin/whats-new.php you will see it is using the Genesis_Admin_Basic class because there are no settings, form, or metabox involved with the page.

A developer could use this to create more advanced integrations with tabs and other UX than are provided in the Genesis admin classes, but it may be better to start with a new abstract class like `Child_Admin_Tabs` to define the basic structure and then extend it so that the code can be reused in the final classes.

One element available in the Genesis admin classes, including the basic class, that has not been discussed is the help system.

help()

Adding a help method will cause the `Genesis_Admin` class to automatically add it as a callback on the `load-{$pagehook}` hook. This can then add help items to the help tab using the `add_help_tab()` method. Technically there is a WordPress method for that and the Genesis method, so let's focus on the Genesis one.

It uses the WordPress method and uses a callback with views. So code like this will add the items if you define the `help_base` property in the class `__construct()` method.

```
/**
 * Contextual help content.
 *
 * @since 2.0.0
 */
public function help() {

        $this->add_help_tab(
'settings', __( 'SEO Settings', 'genesis' ) );
        $this->add_help_tab(
'doctitle', __( 'Doctitle Settings', 'genesis'
) );
        $this->add_help_tab(
'homepage', __( 'Homepage Settings', 'genesis'
) );
        $this->add_help_tab(
```

```
'dochead',    __( 'Document Head Settings',
'genesis' ) );
               $this->add_help_tab(
'robots',    __( 'Robots Meta Settings',
'genesis' ) );

               // Add help sidebar.
               $this->set_help_sidebar();

    }
```

In the `Geneis_Admin_SEO_Settings` class the base is set like this:

```
$this->help_base = GENESIS_VIEWS_DIR . '/help/
seo-';
```

This can be done very similarly to the meta boxes property in the child theme or plugin.

You need to add this to the `__construct()` function for your child theme:

```
$this->views_base = get_stylesheet_directory() .
'/lib/views/help/';
```

If you are using a plugin then this is a good approach:

First, create a constant in the main plugin file like:

```
define(                    'MY_GENESIS_PLUGIN_DIR',
plugin_dir_path( __FILE__ ) );
```

Then you can register your views_base like:

```
$this->views_base   =   MY_GENESIS_PLUGIN_DIR   .
'/lib/views/help/';
```

Again, in either case the files will go into your lib/views/help directory.

WHAT'S NEXT?

Congratulations! This is the end of the core material. You have learned about actions, filters, Genesis functions, and made it through details about Object-oriented programing and Genesis classes. You should be able to add and remove actions and filters as well as find many of the developer tricks available in Genesis.

I love building sites with Genesis and believe you will too.

The next section of the book has some inside tips and tricks that solve some common questions people have when working with Genesis.

PART II.

BONUS

This bonus section has examples taken from tutorials I've written and code I've added to my own themes and plugins.

The examples include documented code that can help you get a jump start on your own theme or plugin. Pay special attention to the Site Recovery Tips and Tricks and the Theme Customization Basic Skills as they will help you with some resources to learn more about PHP, JS, CSS, and HTML as well as how to fix your site if something does go wrong.

CHAPTER 20.

HOW TO RECOVER A CRASHED GENESIS SITE

Something bad is happening on your WordPress site. You try to log in and have a white screen, or the entire site has been replaced with error messages. You're heart is starting to race. Sweat is beading in your face. How will you fix this?

First, calm down. The solution is probably pretty simple. You need to be calm and focused to remember what changes may have led to this. Did you upgrade a plugin, did you install a new plugin, or did you edit your theme functions file? These are the most common issues.

If you are getting a white screen, then please enable debug mode. The white screen is caused by a PHP error and debug mode will tell you what that error is.

If you already have an error, then look and see what it is telling you. Often the errors fit into one of four categories. Either a file is not found, a function is not found, a function is duplicated, or header cannot be modified. These are easy enough to fix.

GENESIS NOT FOUND

The Problem:

One issue that comes up regularly is accidentally activating the child theme without Genesis being installed, or accidentally deleting Genesis (sometimes for a manual upgrade) with the child theme already active. Either of these will result in an error like this

Warning: require_once(%path-to-wordpress%/wp-content/ themes/genesis/lib/init.php) [function.require-once]: failed to open stream: No such file or directory in %path-to-wordpress%/wp-content/themes/%child-theme%/functions.php on line 3

The solution:

You will need to access your site via FTP. Once there, navigate to your site theme directory. This will vary by host and site setup, but it often looks something like this **/public_html/wp-content/themes/**. The error code will actually tell you exactly where this is, but typically you will not have access to the first part of the path. You will have access starting around the public_html(or similar) directory.

If you already have Genesis backed up on your computer, find that folder. Otherwise, you will need to download the latest version of Genesis from StudioPress and unzip. Make a note of where the file is and navigate to it in your FTP client.

Make sure the directory you are about to upload is "genesis" spelled exactly like that and that directly inside the directory is "style.css" (along with several other files and directories). If you are using FileZilla (recommended below) on a Windows system, then right mouse click the "genesis" folder and select to upload. On Mac, you have to activate the context menu by holding ctrl when clicking, unless you have a mouse with a secondary button or other means of accessing the context menu.

The Problem:

When a function doesn't exist, it is often caused by WordPress being out of date. Always upgrade to the latest version of WordPress. Of course, the simple upgrade isn't available if this error happens. The error might look something like this:

> Fatal error: Call to undefined function add_theme_support() in /%path-to-wordpress%/wp-content/themes/genesis/lib/init.php on line 17

The Solution:

You will have to perform a manual upgrade to WordPress. You will need to access your site via FTP.

First, download the latest version of WordPress at wordpress.org and unzip it. Be sure you remember where it is.

Now find your WordPress installation on your site via FTP. It will have several files and at least three folders: wp-admin, wp-content, and wp-includes. First, backup wp-config.php. This is one of your most important files and you don't want to lose it. Now rename wp-admin and wp-includes to **wp-admin-old** and **wp-includes-old**. Find the wordpress folder you unzipped and open it. You should see the same folders are you have on your site. Select everything except the wp-content directory. In FileZilla this can be done quickly with "ctrl+a" then holding "ctrl" and clicking on wp-content to unselect. Now right click and select upload.

You will get a message asking if you wish to overwrite the files. Select yes. In FileZilla you can select to do this for all of the files and to limit it to that queue only. I recommend those settings when answering yes to save time.

After all files are uploaded, go to your site dashboard to complete the upgrade. You should get a screen asking if you want to upgrade the database. Do that and the site should be working correctly.

PROBLEMS WITH PLUGINS

The Problem:

It is always a good idea to disable plugins when upgrading WordPress. Often a plugin will be perfectly stable in one version of WordPress and break another version completely. If you have an error message pointing to a specific plugin, you can just disable that plugin. Otherwise you may have to troubleshoot the site by disabling all plugins. There are a lot of errors that can be caused by plugins, including plugins that define a function already defined in Genesis or the Child theme, or bad coding in the plugin that results in an error. An error message might look like:

> Warning: Cannot modify header information – headers already sent by (output started at /%path-to-wordpress%/wp-content/plugins/%plugin-folder%/%plugin-file%.php:119) in /%path-to-wordpress%/wp-login.php on line 337

The Solution:

You will need to access your site via FTP.

If you have a specific fatal error for a specific plugin, then navigate to that plugin. It will be in your plugins directory. This is specific to your host and WordPress installation, but it often looks like **/public_html/wp-content/plugins/**. Now rename the plugin directory to "directory-name-disabled." For example, if you have a plugin called "foo" in the directory "foo" then you need to change the directory name to **foo-disabled**.

If you do not know exactly which plugin is causing the problem, or are troubleshooting to see if plugins are causing the problem, then rename the entire plugins folder to **plugins-disabled**. If this resolved the problem, then you need to identify the problem plugin. Go to your site and access the plugins page. Make sure everything is disabled then rename your folder back to **plugins**. Now activate half of your plugins. If the error comes back you know the bad plugin is in that half, if not it is in the other half. Keep activating and deactivating in halves to narrow the error down to a specific plugin. Any time the site goes down you will know there is a bad plugin activated, but you will also have to disable the plugins again via FTP to get your site back.

ERROR IN CHILD THEME EDIT

The Problem:

You were making a change to your theme and now everything is broken. These errors fall into several classes, but the most common are bad php, mixing html with php, and "header already sent." This last error might look like this:

> Warning: Cannot modify header information – headers already sent by (output started at /%path-to-wordpress%/wp-content/themes/%child-theme%/functions.php:119) in /%path-to-wordpress%/wp-login.php on line 337

The Solution:

You will need to access your site via FTP. (Getting repetitive isn't it?)

For bad php or mixing php with html, you need to restore that file from a backup. Ask on the forums how to properly format your php.

For the header already sent error, this is almost always caused by something before the first `<?php` or after the last `?>` in the file. technically you don't need that last `?>` and the child themes are removing that to minimize this type of error. Find the file using the FTP client and right click to "view/edit." If prompted for a program use notepad. If your file ends with a ?> delete it. If anything is before the first <?php, even empty space such as a space or return delete and then upload the file.

HOW TO ACCESS YOUR SITE VIA FTP

To access your site via FTP, you will need a few things.

First, a FTP client. I recommend FileZilla. It is free (that should be enough right there), works on any operating system, and has a lot of helpful features.

Second, you must have login credentials for your site. This includes the host, which is often your url, the username, and password. If you do not know any of these, the company you are hosting your site with can provide the details.

Filezilla is easy to use. The default setup shows a split pane (right and left) for your computer and your site. The files and folders on the left are your computer, and the files and folders on the right are your site. This can be navigated by typing in the location in the field next to "Local site:" or "Remote site:" or via the folder tree directly under that field. You may also double click on folders to open them in the bottom of the split pane. The ".." directory takes you up one level.

ACTIVATING DEBUG MODE

You will need to access your site via FTP. Once there, go to the directory that WordPress is installed in. You should see the wp-config.php file. This file may already have this line of code.

```
define('WP_DEBUG', false );
```

If so, just change "false" to "true" and update the file. Otherwise, add this before the stop editing line (I am showing that line in this code example to give you in idea of where to place it, no need to add that line again).

```
define('WP_DEBUG', true );

/* That's all, stop editing! Happy blogging. */
```

Once you update the file, you may see quite a few errors. The most important error is the last 1-2 errors, these are the ones being generated just before things break completely.

After you are done fixing your site, be sure to change the "true" back to false.

CHAPTER 21.

HOW TO CREATE PAGE TEMPLATES IN GENESIS

A question I field on a regular basis is "How do I make a page template in Genesis?" It's actually very easy to do, and I have a template I want to share for my Production theme.

Two users in a day asked how to combine videos and posts into a single blog view. Merging post types is pretty simple, you just need a custom loop. However, for people that are new to Genesis, making the page template can feel daunting. Hopefully this article will make it much less so.

STEP 1: CREATE THE FILE

You will need to add a new file to your child theme folder. It must be a PHP file, and must be in the same directory as the style.css and functions.php files. The name isn't strictly speaking important, but if you look in the Genesis directory you will find two page template files named page_archive.php and page_blog.php. I personally recommend using this same pattern because it makes it easy to identify what your template files are at a glance and helps to remind you what the file does.

For this specific template, please make the new file page_video_blog.php and upload it to the child theme directory. If you aren't sure how to make a new php file, follow these simple steps.

- Start a basic text editor, like Notepad (alternately you can use an advanced editor like Notepad++ or Netbeans, but if you know about those you probably don't need these instructions).

- Add your code (which we will discuss later).

- Use the "save as" menu option and be sure to select "all" file types then type in page_video_blog.php, or whatever name you will be using.

STEP 2: NAME YOUR TEMPLATE

WordPress will scan every PHP file in the theme directory (the same level as the style.css and functions.php) for some specific code. That code makes your template work. Fortunately, this is super easy. For the sake of this tutorial, put this at the top of your file.

```php
<?php
/*
* Template Name: Video Blog
*/
```

The first line starts with PHP. The next three lines are a PHP comment. This doesn't run any actual code, but WordPress is looking for it. The "Template Name:" part is what clues WordPress in on what this file is, and "Video Blog" will be the name used to identify your template. You can see it in the Page Attributes image on the right.

Page Attributes

Parent

(no parent) ▼

Template

Video Blog ▼

Order

0

Need help? Use the Help tab in the upper right of your screen.

STEP 3: USE ACTIONS AND FILTERS TO CHANGE THE PAGE OUTPUT

This is the real guts of the page template. As I said, two different people asked about adding Videos and Posts to a single blog template,so I am showing how to build that template. This code goes after the Template Name code and comprises the rest of the file.

```
/**
* This removes the loop.
* If you want to include the static page title
and content,
* remove or comment out this code.
*/
remove_action( 'genesis_loop',
'genesis_do_loop' );

add_action( 'genesis_loop',
'child_do_video_blog_loop' );
/**
```

```
* This builds the video blog loop.
* The blog options in the Genesis Theme
Settings are applied.
* A custom field on the page with the name
query_args can be used.
* This will change the posts and videos pulled
into the loop.
* By default it will pull in all posts and
videos.
*/
function child_do_video_blog_loop() {

$include = genesis_get_option( 'blog_cat' );
$exclude = genesis_get_option(
'blog_cat_exclude' ) ? explode( ',',
str_replace( ' ', '', genesis_get_option(
'blog_cat_exclude' ) ) ) : '';
$paged = get_query_var( 'paged' ) ?
get_query_var( 'paged' ) : 1;

/** Easter Egg */
$query_args = wp_parse_args(
genesis_get_custom_field( 'query_args' ),
array(
'cat' => $include,
'category__not_in' => $exclude,
'showposts' => genesis_get_option(
'blog_cat_num' ),
'paged' => $paged,
'post_type' => array( 'post', 'video')
)
);

genesis_custom_loop( $query_args );
```

```
}

//loads the framework
genesis();
```

You can see an example of this code output here. Notice that the first post in the image is a post, and the second is a video):

Kid Rock Joins Bon Jovi in London

01.15.12 By rockthegeek * Leave a Comment (Edit)

This is an example of a WordPress post, you could edit this to put information about yourself or your site so readers know where you are coming from. You can create as many posts as you like in order to share with your readers what exactly is on your mind. This is an example of a WordPress post... [Read more...]

Filed Under: Music News

Sample Video #1

01.10.12 By rockthegeek * Leave a Comment (Edit)

This is an example of a WordPress post, you could edit this to put information about yourself or your site so readers know where you are coming from. You can create as many posts as you like in order to share with your readers what exactly is on your mind. This is an example of a WordPress post... [Read more...]

CHAPTER 22.

HOW TO VERSION YOUR GENESIS STYLESHEET

One helpful, but also frustrating, feature of modern development is cached stylesheets.

Cached styles are a good thing and I would never want to disable them, but if I make a change on my site and a user has a cached version of my style sheet, things won't look right. The viewer can do a hard refresh in their browser, but that's asking a lot, especially for changes on my site.

That's why I version my stylesheet. The code is really simple and it lets me update the style sheet the world sees when they visit my site. Right now, this is what it looks like in my functions.php file:

```
remove_action('genesis_meta',
'genesis_load_stylesheet');
add_action('genesis_meta',
'ntg_load_stylesheet');
/**
* Loads Versions Style Sheet
*
* @uses wp_enqueue_style()
* @author Nick the Geek
*
*/
```

```
function ntg_load_stylesheet() {

wp_enqueue_style( 'ntg-style',
get_bloginfo('stylesheet_url'), array(),
'1.0.1.4', 'screen' );


}
```

If I make a CSS change I need to push to the world, I can change "1.0.1.4" to "1.0.1.5".

Another method that will make the version update automatically when the file is changed is to use a timestamp for when the file was modified.

```
remove_action('genesis_meta',
'genesis_load_stylesheet');
add_action('genesis_meta',
'ntg_load_stylesheet');
/**
* Loads Versions Style Sheet
*
* @uses wp_enqueue_style()
* @author Nick the Geek
*
*/
function ntg_load_stylesheet() {

wp_enqueue_style( 'ntg-style',
get_bloginfo('stylesheet_url'), array(),
filemtime( get_stylesheet_directory() .
'/style.css' ), 'screen' );


}
```

This will cause the version to update automatically every time the file is updated.

CHAPTER 23.

HOW TO ADD A WIDGET AREA TO GENESIS

One question I have answered repeatedly is, "How do you add a new widgeted area to Genesis?"

With a little bit of code this can be handled with relative ease.

You will be editing the functions.php file, so make sure you have a backup of the file and a way to access your site via FTP, not just the theme editor in the dashboard. If you aren't sure how to access your site via FTP, please contact your host before continuing this tutorial. They should be able to provide FTP login details. You also need an FTP client like Filezilla, which is free and available for every major operating system.

You also need to know a couple of important functions.

- "genesis_register_widget_area()" will register the sidebar.
- "genesis_widget_area()" will display the sidebar.

There are several ways to use these functions, but for the sake of simplicity, this tutorial will only cover basic usage.

IMPORTANT TERMS

There are a few important terms used in this article

- Sidebar/Widgeted Area: These terms refer to the exact same thing. Often there is confusion when "sidebar" is used because people assume that it can only mean a portion of the site alongside the content. In both cases, it means any area of the site that uses widgets to display content.

- Widget: This is a WordPress tool that allows users to change and rearrange the content in sidebars. There are several default widgets included with WordPress. Additionally, themes and plugins may add to or replace the default widgets. This allows for significant customization from the site administrator.

REGISTER YOUR WIDGET AREA

Open your functions.php file to register a new sidebar. Most child themes probably have a few sidebars registered at the bottom of the file. This code can go after the existing code, or at the bottom of the file if there aren't any sidebars currently registered. You will be using this code.

```
genesis_register_widget_area( array(
    'id'            => 'after-content-ad',
    'name'          => __( 'After Content Ad',
'child' ),
    'description' => __( 'This is a sidebar
that goes after the content.', 'child' ),
) );
```

These are the three most important options.

- The "id" must be a unique ID and uses all lower case, no special characters, or spaces. You can use numbers.
- The "name" is more flexible, you can use spaces and other characters. This identifies the widget area in the dashboard.
- The "description" is used in the dashboard to help describe where the widget area will be used.

You can register however many widget areas your theme will need using this function over and over. It is very important that each widget area have a unique "id" and to limit confusion, the "name" should also be different for each widget area you make.

DISPLAY YOUR WIDGET AREA

Now that you have a widget area registered, you need to call for the widget area. In this example, we will be loading the widget area after the content and any sidebars, so an add can be inserted via a text widget below the content and sidebars. You can use the Genesis Hook Reference in the first chapter to pick the right hook for inserting the widget area. This tutorial will be using the "genesis_after_content_sidebar_wrap" hook. This code will go in the functions.php file.

```
add_action(
'genesis_after_content_sidebar_wrap',
'child_after_content_ad_sidebar' );
/**
 * Loads a new sidebar after the content
 */
function child_after_content_ad_sidebar() {
        genesis_widget_area( 'after-content-ad'
array(
                'before' => genesis_markup(
array(
                        'open'    => '<aside
class="widget-area after-content-ad">',
                        'context' =>
'widget-area-wrap',
                        'echo'    => false,
                        'params'  => array(
                                'id' => $id,
                        ),
                ) ),
```

```
        ) );
}
```

If you prefer to use the Genesis Simple Hooks plugin at this point, add this to the "genesis_after_content_sidebar_wrap" field (make sure you enable PHP on that hook).

```php
<?php
        genesis_widget_area ( 'after-content-ad'
array (
                'before' => genesis_markup (
array (
                        'open'    => '<aside
class="widget-area">',
                        'context' =>
'widget-area-wrap',
                        'echo'    => false,
                        'params'  => array (
                                'id' => $id,
                        ),
                ) ),
        ) );
?>
```

STYLE YOUR WIDGET AREA

This is the most subjective part of this tutorial. You might need to make several rules to control how it is displayed on your site and how different widgets look inside your specific widget area. Since this tutorial is about adding a widgeted area not CSS, this section is only going to cover the most basic CSS rules to show how it works. This widget area is supposed to be a spot for a banner ad after the content and sidebar. I'm going to apply a clear, which will prevent the various floats used for the content, sidebars, and content sidebar wrap from affecting how this ad space works. I'm also going ot set a specific max-width, for 728px banner ads, and center it with auto margin. This also has 20px top and bottom margin to give it some breathing room. Depending on the theme this might need more.

The fixed max-width combined with the 100% width will make the container responsive. So it will be the full width of the screen until the screen is more than 728px wide.

Open your style sheet (typically style.css) and add this to the bottom of the file.

```
/* Ad Sidebar
--------------------------------------------------
------------ */
.after-content-ad {
    clear: both;
    margin: 20px auto;
    width: 100%;
    max-width: 728px;
}
```

That's it. If you followed these steps you now have a new sidebar in the dashboard. Put a text widget in with ad code for a 728px wide ad and you are done.

ADDITIONAL EXAMPLES

It is straightforward to add a new widget area to Genesis child themes. Now you can take this code, and with a few small changes adapt it to any part of the theme. Since some people learn by doing, grab the sample child theme and play with adding new sidebars all over the theme. Other people learn by examples, so here are three more widget areas you can use in your theme. Note the simple differences that make a big difference in where the widget areas go.

Ad widget area above header

Start by registering a new widget area in the functions.php file

```
genesis_register_widget_area( array(
    'id'            => 'before-header-ad',
    'name'          => __( 'Before Header Ad',
'child' ),
    'description' => __( 'This is a sidebar
that goes before the header.', 'child' ),
) );
```

Next, display your widget area using this code in the functions.php file.

```
add_action( 'genesis_before',
'child_before_header_ad_widget_area' );
/**
 *Loads a new widget area before the #wrap
 */
function child_before_header_ad_widget_area() {
        genesis_widget_area( 'before-header-ad'
array(
                'before' => genesis_markup(
array(
                        'open'     => '<aside
class="widget-area">',
                        'context' =>
'widget-area-wrap',
                        'echo'     => false,
                        'params'   => array(
                                'id' => $id,
                        ),
                ) ),
        ) );
}
```

Finally, style your Widget Area using this code in the style.css file:

```css
/* Ad Sidebar
---------------------------------------------------
------------ */

.before-header-ad {
    clear: both;
    margin: 20px auto;
    max-width: 728px;
    width: 100%;
}
```

Widget Area Before Posts

Start by registering a new widget area in the functions.php file:

```php
genesis_register_widget_area( array(
    'id'            => 'before-posts-sidebar',
    'name'          => __( 'Before Posts',
'child' ),
    'description' => __( 'This is a sidebar
that goes before the posts in the #content.',
'child' ),
) );
```

Next, display your widget area using this code in the functions.php file.

```php
add_action( 'genesis_before_loop',
'child_before_posts_sidebar' );
/**
 * Loads a new sidebar before the posts in the
#content
 */
```

```php
function child_before_posts_sidebar() {
        genesis_widget_area(
'before-posts-sidebar' array(
                'before' => genesis_markup(
array(
                        'open'     => '<aside
class="widget-area before-posts-sidebar">',
                        'context' =>
'widget-area-wrap',
                        'echo'     => false,
                        'params'   => array(
                                'id' => $id,
                        ),
                ) ),
        ) );
}
```

Finally, style your widget area using this code in the style.css file:

```css
/* Before Posts
----------------------------------------------
------------ */

.before-posts-sidebar {
    background: #dddddd;
    padding: 10px;
}
```

After Post Subscribe Box

Start by registering a new widget area in the functions.php file:

```php
genesis_register_sidebar( array(
    'id'            => 'after-post-box',
    'name'          => __( 'After Post Box',
'child' ),
```

```
    'description' => __( 'This is a sidebar
that goes after the posts for a subscribe
box.', 'child' ),
) );
```

Next, display your sidebar using this code in the functions.php
file. Note this also includes an "if()" statement, so it only shows
on the single post page.

```
add_action( 'genesis_after_entry_content',
'child_after_post_box' );
/**
 * Loads a new sidebar after the post on single
pages
 */
function child_after_post_box() {

        if ( is_single() ) {
                genesis_widget_area(
'after-content-ad' array(
                        'before' =>
genesis_markup( array(
                                'open'     =>
'<aside class="widget-area">',
                                'context' =>
'widget-area-wrap',
                                'echo'     =>
false,
                                'params'   =>
array(
                                        'id' =>
$id,
                                ),
                        ) ),
                ) );
```

```
            }
}
```

Finally, style your sidebar using this code in the style.css file:

```
/* After Post Box
------------------------------------------------
------------ */

.after-post-box {
    clear: both;
    margin: 10px;
    border: 1px dotted #777777;
    padding: 10px;
}
```

CHAPTER 24.

HOW TO CHANGE THE CONTENT LIMIT IN GENESIS

Here is a quick tip about changing the content limit in Genesis for specific categories, archives, or other content area. The content limit refers to how many characters appear on the screen.

Genesis has a ton of filters and actions, but if you go look in the genesis/lib/structure/post.php file at the "genesis_do_post_content()" function, you will find that you cannot change the content limit because there isn't a filter there ... or is there?

You will actually have to look in the genesis/lib/functions/options.php file at the "genesis_get_option()" function. There is a "genesis_pre_get_ filter" that lets you change the option if you want. This is a super cool filter that lets you make changes all over the place.

I'm going to share a code snippet to change the content limit.

```
add_filter(
'genesis_pre_get_option_content_archive_limit',
'my_content_archive_limit' );
/**
```

```
 * Changes the content limit for a specific
category.
 *
 * @param int $limit The current limit.
 *
 * @return int The new limit.
 */
function my_content_archive_limit( $limit ) {
    //replace "x" with your category ID.
    if ( is_category('x') ) {
        // Character based not word based.
        $limit = 1000;
    }

    return $limit;
}
```

Now maybe you want to do this for a post type archive at 500 characters, all tags at 700 characters, and category "x" at 100 characters. I don't know why you want to do that, but you could use this instead:

```
add_filter(
'genesis_pre_get_option_content_archive_limit',
'my_content_archive_limit' );
/**
 * Changes the content limit for a specific
category.
 *
 * @param int $limit The current limit.
 *
 * @return int The new limit.
 */
function my_content_archive_limit( $limit ) {
    if ( is_category('219') ) {
        $limit = 1000;
```

```
    } elseif ( is_tag() ) {
        $limit = 750;
    } elseif ( is_archive() && 'my_post_type'
== get_post_type() ) {
        $limit = 500;
    }

    return $limit;
}
```

You can target pretty much any archive or combination of archives with the right conditionals.

CHAPTER 25.

HOW TO LOAD A NEW SECTION ON SPECIFIC PAGES

Often it is desirable to put a new section into a site, but only in certain places or under certain circumstances. This is a relatively simple process and may be done via a theme function or from the Genesis Simple Hooks plugin.

For both of these examples, I will just display "hello world" before the loop so I need the "genesis_before_loop" hook. If I wanted to display this elsewhere, I would use another hook. I also need to know the conditional tags built into WordPress. The most common ones are:

- **is_home()** – Returns true on home page.
- **is_front_page()** – Returns true on front page.
- **is_singular()** – Returns true on single post or page.
- **is_page()** – Returns true on single page.
- **is_single()** – Returns true on single post.
- **in_category()** – Returns true if post is in a category.
- **has_tag()** – Returns true if a post has a tag.
- **is_category()** – Returns true on category.
- **is_archive()** – Returns true on any archive.

You will see that there are a lot of other options in the WordPress codex article, including additional arguments for selecting specific categories, pages and posts.

Using them with hooks is not too difficult. If you want to put "<h3>Hello World</h3>" at the top of all of your pages, then you could paste that into your function, or into the "genesis_before_loop" field of Genesis Simple Hooks.

What if you only want this to show up on the home page? Put in a conditional tag.

This is what you would paste into your function when adding a section with hooks:

```
add_action( 'genesis_before_loop',
'child_before_loop' );
/**
 * Adds "Hello World" before the loop on the
home page.
 */
function child_before_loop() {
    if ( is_home() ) {
?>
        <h3>Hello World</h3>
<?php
    }
}
```

The only difference between Genesis Simple Hooks and the add to site via hooks method is you need to enable PHP on the hook and in your code. So, if I were using Genesis Simple Hooks, this is what I would paste into the field to have my code only show up on pages.

```
<?php if ( is_page() ) : ?>
```

```
<h3>Hello World</h3>
<?php endif; ?>
```

This would work the exact same for any post, page, category …
so long as there is a conditional tag for it, but what if I want this
to show on posts in category "foo" or on a page? Use this code
(don't forget the php tags if using GSH):

```
add_action( 'genesis_before_loop',
'child_before_loop' );
/**
 * Adds "Hello World" before the loop on any
page or posts in category "foo".
 */
function child_before_loop() {
    if ( is_page() || in_category('foo') ) {
?>
        <h3>Hello World</h3>
<?php
    }
}
```

The "||" is like saying "or", so the code will run if either of those
tags return true. However, sometimes you want something to
run if both tags are true. Maybe you have posts that are in
category "foo" and are tagged with "bar". You can do this:

```
add_action( 'genesis_before_loop',
'child_before_loop' );
/**
 * Adds "Hello World" before the loop on any
posts in category "foo" that is also tagged
with "bar".
 */
function child_before_loop() {
    if ( in_category('foo') &amp;&amp;
```

```
has_tag('bar') ) {
?>
        <h3>Hello World</h3>
<?php
    }
}
```

This will only show "Hello World" on posts in the category that also have the tag. "&&" is like saying "and".

Finally, there are times you do not want to add something to your site everywhere, but you want to add it to a specific part of the site. For example, you want to say "Hello World" on pages, posts, categories … but not the home page. Then make this small change to the first code:

```
add_action( 'genesis_before_loop',
'child_before_loop' );
/**
 * Adds "Hello World" before the loop on any
page, post, or archive that is not the home
page.
 */
function child_before_loop() {
    if ( ! is_home() ) {
?>
        <h3>Hello World</h3>
<?php
    }
}
```

That little "!" tells the code to return the opposite of normal. Another way of thinking of it is "!" = "not". Our conditional tag is saying "If this is not the home page, then echo **Hello World**."

The conditional tag is very powerful and can be extended to long complex strings.

CHAPTER 26.

HOW TO BUILD A GENESIS PLUGIN

Life is full of firsts and movies like to make "first" experiences look so good. The movie *50 First Dates* has a line where Drew Barrymore's character says,

"There is nothing like a first kiss."

Princess Diaries has a subplot point that revolves around a first kiss and how it should make your foot "pop".

I hope first experience with building plugins can be equally exciting!

I had a lot of help with my first plugin, and that plugin has since become fairly popular. However, I did several revisions to clean up code. I also added features. Nonetheless, I want to do a full overhaul on the plugin, because when I look at the code, I keep asking, "Why did I do it like that?"

I think a lot of developers do the same thing. We end up with a lot of plugins hat need an overhaul, but we've moved on and learned so much that it is almost painful to think about that first awkward plugin. I'm going to share some tips and ideas I've learned over the years. Hopefully with these tips and ideas, you'll learn something to make your first or current plugins even better.

If you want a complete class on building plugins, check out these courses: https://ostraining.com/classes/wordpress-development/.

WHY BUILD A PLUGIN?

Some of you already have a great idea and know it is going to be the best possible plugin ever, but there are folks reading this that don't think of themselves as a plugin developer. They make themes and that is good enough.

Listen, if you don't want to build a plugin ever, that's fine. I'm not going to look down on you and think you are an inferior developer. We're cool. That said, you might want to keep reading because there are reasons for theme developers to learn to build good plugins too.

Theme features that aren't theme specific

Bill Erickson got me started on the idea that theme developers should be making these core functionality plugins instead of building everything into their custom themes. He writes on this in more detail, and in turn links to other developers who have written in even more detail. It's a rabbit hole that just keeps going.

The short version is, features you might add to a site for a client like custom fields, custom post types, and short codes are part of the site, not the theme. If the client ever changed themes, they would lose those features. That would be bad for the site. If you are developing themes for clients or even for yourself, I'd recommend building core functionality plugins to pull some features into the plugin instead of the theme.

Here's an example by experience. I added a lot of cool features to my site, and each time I'd change themes, I had to find the code and transfer it to the new theme. This caused a lot of frustration while changing themes. After Bill talked about this type of feature with me, I decided to start moving features to the core functionality plugin. Now 75% or more of the features built into my site have been moved to the plugin. Only CSS and sidebars are really part of my theme. This has made it much easier any time I change themes, because I just focus on design, knowing my functionality is there.

Repeat Features

Clients love to think they are being cutting edge and unique, but 90% of the time clients give me a link to some cool thing they saw that they want on their site. The truth is, the more clients I have, the more I find I'm doing a lot of the same thing. Part of building a good core functionality plugin is learning what repeated things you are doing and build that for easy access. I can build out a custom project for a client, and it might take 40 hours because I built ever line from scratch. The next client will do some similar things and I already know what I'm doing, so it may only take 30 hours or even less time. If I'm noticing that I keep getting asked for a portfolio, I can build a portfolio plugin. Then I include that for the client and focus on styling instead of having to develop a new portfolio for each client separately.

It saves me time, saves them money, and makes my development more consistent. The truth is, most of the features I built into plugins, like the Genesis Featured Widget Extended, were because of needs I had to make something for a client. I didn't want to have to build a completely custom widget.

You have a great idea

I think most publicly released plugins probably fall under this. The movie *Robots* has a recurring line, "See a need, fill a need." I think that is the heart of what WordPress plugin developers are all about. We often see things that need to happen and then ignore them because we assume that someone more skilled will make it happen … eventually. The truth is, if you see a need you can fill the need. Build your first plugin and then learn from it. You don't have to be perfect the first time out. I know I wasn't. Shoot, I often build out plugins for Copyblogger and find that it needs a lot of polish when I thought it was done. That's ok.

If you have an idea for a plugin, it is time to make it happen.

BUILD YOUR PLUGIN

So you are ready to make your first plugin … now what? The developer who helped me get my first plugin out the door is Gary Jones. I think he would say the first thing you need to do is learn some code standards.

Why are code standards important?

The short answer is, so your code doesn't suck.

Code standards mean your code is easier to read, easier to understand, and easier to fix.

PHP is a very forgiving language. You can do a lot of weird things in PHP that you can't in other languages. Sure, when it breaks it is more cryptic about why things are broken, but relatively speaking, you have to work harder to break it. That doesn't mean that you should just go hog wild because you can.

By learning to use proper white spacing, formatting, and documentation you will be better serving your users and (more importantly) your future self.

I'm at the point where I will sketch up ideas for a plugin then sit down and write. I can write up multiple files with hundreds of lines of code each then debug it. When I first started I had to run things in smaller chunks, but now I can conceptualize the entire project because I've done it often enough. When I debug, things are bound to be broken though. So I'll have to go in and find the issues and fix them.

Proper white spacing means it is easier to read the code. Using smaller functions means it is easier to follow what is happening, and documenting as I go along means I will remember what I was thinking when I wrote a given bit of code.

Since WordPress and Genesis plugins mean you are working with other standards, you need to learn those standards so you are compliant with that system. By doing so, someone who is familiar with reading WordPress code will be able to quickly read your code. It also means your plugin is more likely to work with the themes and plugins others have developed.

WordPress has a pretty good resource on coding standards for contributing to WP core.

After you have the basics down, check out the WordPress Plugin Developer Handbook.

Once you learn the standards and are ready to build, you will need to create your plugin.

Minimum requirements for a plugin

For your first plugin you need at least one PHP file and a readme.txt file. Many simple plugins use a single PHP file, and there is no specific reason you need multiple files. That said, if your plugin will be using admin, front end, and general functions, it may be good to break it up into separate files.

By moving functions to different files and loading them conditionally, you make it easier to quickly identify what various parts of your code do. You make it load fewer resources at any given time. This may only result in a few milliseconds per page load in added speed, but on a busy server that can be a pretty important savings.

Use Genesis Init for Genesis plugins

I see a lot of Genesis-specific plugins, and most of them are pretty cool. The great thing about Genesis is the way it is built to be extended by child themes **and** plugins. I love that developers out there take things they think are cool and make very helpful plugins.

That said; folks, you got to use "genesis_init".

This hook is loaded on the WordPress init action. The biggest difference between loading your plugin on the "init" hook and the "genesis_init" hook is the later only exists if Genesis is being used. It is a super efficient way of making sure any "genesis_" function is going to be available. Now, this doesn't take the place of checking to make sure a function is available, but if you run a version comparison, you can know what functions and classes are available to you on the "genesis_init" hook.

> It isn't enough to do a theme check when you activate the plugin.

When you do a theme check while activating your plugin, you only know that the theme functions are available at the time the plugin is activated. If users switch themes, you can white screen their site. More importantly, if they are using a tool that disables the theme in certain circumstances, you can white screen their site.

For example, let's say someone is using JetPack. I'm not going to argue if this is a good or bad thing, but it is a popular tool so many users have it active. Jetpack activates a mobile theme by default. Again, I'm not saying this is good or **very, very bad**, but a lot of people don't know and leave it active. If your plugin loads on the "init" hook and you don't carefully check to make sure all of your Genesis functions are available before using them, people visiting the site via a mobile device will see a lovely white screen.

For safety, please use the "genesis_init" hook when loading your plugin actions.

Example plugin file

Here is an example from a plugin I recently finished. I've added inline documentation to help explain everything:

```
<?php
/*
Plugin Name: Genesis Boilerplate
Plugin URI:
Description: A Simple plugin template used for
building other plugins.
Version: 0.1.0
Author: Nick_theGeek
Author URI: http://designsbynickthegeek.com
Text Domain: genesis-boilerplate
Domain Path /languages/

*/

/*
The previous section is what defines the plugin.
The Plugin Name line defines the name.
The Plugin URI line is a link to where the
plugin details can be found online
Since this plugin isn't released I'm just
linking to root domain
The Description line is the short description
that will show in the WordPress dashboard.
The Version line defines the version of the
plugin file
```

The Author line defines the author. This should match your WordPress user name if uploading to the WordPress repo
The Author URI provides a link to your Web site
The text domain line allow you to hint at the domain that is used for internationalizing your text strings
The domain path defines where WordPress should look for translation files.
*/

/* Prevent direct access to the plugin */
if (!defined('ABSPATH')) {
die("Sorry, you are not allowed to access this page directly.");
}

/* I like to define a constant for the /lib/ and other directories so I don't have to call dirname() all the time */
define('GENESIS_BOILERPLATE_LIB', dirname(__FILE__) . '/lib/');

/*
One thing I'm skipping in this plugin is an activation hook action. This type of action loads when your plugin
is activated. That is when you would want to check to see what version of Genesis is being used.
I'm only using the genesis_get_option and genesis_get_image functions in this plugin. Those functions have been available for all public releases of Genesis so I'm just using the genesis_init hook.

```
It's a bit of a cheat but it works and I hate
loading code that I don't absolutely need.
If I were doing something with functions that
were added in 2.0 or something I'd run an
activation hook or
I'd do a "function exists" before continuing.
*/


/*
Notice that this is loaded on genesis_init. If
this was not a Genesis specific plugin I could
just load on init
Since I loaded on genesis_init I know certain
Genesis functions like genesis_get_option will
be available
Also note that I have name spaced the function
I created with "genesis_boilerplate" so I don't
conflict with other plugins
*/
add_action( 'genesis_init',
'genesis_boilerplate_init', 99 );
/**
* Loads plugin text domain and required files.
Uses genesis_init to ensure Genesis functions
are available
*
* @since 0.1.0
*
* @uses GENESIS_BOILERPLATE_LIB
*
*/
function genesis_boilerplate_init() {

/** Load textdomain for translation */
load_plugin_textdomain( 'genesis-boilerplate',
```

```
false, basename( dirname( __FILE__ ) ) .
'/languages/' );

/*
Checks to see if this is an admin screen and if
the Genesis_Admin_Boxes class is available
Since the admin class is not part of Genesis
1.0 I do a check here to make sure it is there
I could have done the activation check to make
sure Genesis 1.8 or higher was running but I
went with this class_exists() check instead
*/
if ( is_admin() && class_exists(
'Genesis_Admin_Boxes' ) ) {
require_once( GENESIS_BOILERPLATE_LIB .
'admin.php' );
}
else { //if this is not an admin screen it is
the front end and the appropriate files are
loaded
require_once( GENESIS_BOILERPLATE_LIB .
'front-end.php' );
}

//this plugin doesn't load any common functions
but if it did I would uncomment this line
//require_once( GENESIS_BOILERPLATE_LIB .
'functions.php' );

}
```

CHAPTER 27.

HOW TO BUILD A WORDPRESS ADMIN PAGE WITH GENESIS

When it comes to admin pages, you need to start with a plan.

You may already know what you want your plugin to do, but what options do you want to make for the plugin users? The way I see it, there are two schools of thought on this.

- Add all the options.
- Add minimal to no options.

Each of these approaches are based on different underlying opinions on what a user wants. If you go ask a user if they want more options, they will probably say, "yes". We like the idea of control, so we want more ways to control the output.

A lot of studies in UX/UI seem to point towards users actually preferring fewer and more intuitive options. A great example is the iOS. People love it because it is simple and easy to use. Sure, you are much more limited in what you can do, but most users just don't care so long as it works.

Regardless of which approach you follow, I highly recommend outlining the options, then reviewing them to ask if they make sense. I tend to add all the options to my initial outline, then I start asking myself how I can condense the options. A few lucky people have been able to get in on some early testing for the Genesis Simple Share plugin. I hope they really like the super simple admin UI. When it started there were several options for each sharing icon and then some additional general options. In the end, the sharing icons were mostly given a single option, "enable this icon". The interface was cleaned up, and I think it is much easier for people to use.

For "power" users who might want to have more complex control, it is possible to use template functions to do a lot more.

I personally think that is how we should approach the admin. If you can make your plugin work well without user controlled settings, skip this article. Of course, most of the time you need to have at least some options, but consider making a minimalist admin page. Include only what is necessary, especially for your initial release.

As a closing example, I run sound for my church. I was watching videos to learn more about how to balance the sound because I noticed that often, the live mix seemed muddy and harsh. One sound technician said "Always cut first." What that means is, when mixing sound, you need to find the frequencies that sound bad and lower those for each instrument and vocalist first. This creates places for other sounds to fill and makes it a lot easier to bring up a few things to round out the sound than to have too much stacked in a small frequency range. That is what makes muddy and harsh sounding music. The next week I did a lot of cuts and did very little else to change the mix. The music was significantly better than the prior week.

I think we, as developers, have a habit of filling the voids because we can, but that results in overwhelming option screens that are hard to use. Try cutting options first, then add back anything you absolutely need.

ADD THE PAGE

Now that you have an idea of what options you will need it is time to build your page. There are quite a few good tutorials on working with the Genesis admin class. This was introduced in Genesis 1.8 and has made it very easy to build a consistent admin experience across plugins. This is important because a consistent experience means users will be more likely to know how your admin screen works. After all, they have already seen similar screens.

That said, if you can come up with an intuitive way to get your options on page, then take time to work on added styling and js. I've been seeing some users that have done some really interesting things lately like the Genesis Design Palette Pro plugin by Reaktiv Studios (Funny story, years after I originally wrote that line, I work for Reaktiv Studios).

Here is what the basic class looks like with the bare essentials in place. I'll fill those in as I explain the various parts in more detail.

```php
<?php
/**
 * Creates the plugin admin page.
 *
 *
 * @category Genesis Boilerplate
 * @package Admin
 * @author copyblogger
 * @license http://www.opensource.org/licenses/
gpl-license.php GPL-2.0+
 */

/* Prevent direct access to the plugin */
if ( !defined( 'ABSPATH' ) ) {
        die( "Sorry, you are not allowed to
```

```php
access this page directly." );
}

/**
 * Registers a new admin page, providing content
 * and corresponding menu items
 *
 * @category Genesis Boilerplate
 * @package Admin
 *
 * @since 0.1.0
 */
class Genesis_Boilerplate_Boxes extends
Genesis_Admin_Boxes {

        /**
         * Create an admin menu item and
settings page.
         *
         * @since 0.1.0
         *
         */
        function __construct() {

                /*
                Defines the setting value.
                You will use
genesis_get_option( 'option',
'genesis_boilerplate' );
                to retrieve "option" from this
field later
                */
                $settings_field =
'genesis_boilerplate';
```

```
                //allows you to set defaults.
Look for a full example below
                $default_settings = array();

                //define where your page can be
found
                $menu_ops = array(
                'submenu' => array(
                        /** Do not use without
'main_menu' */
                        'parent_slug' =>
'genesis', //loads under "genesis" menu
                        'page_title' => __(
'Genesis Boilerplate Settings',
'genesis-boilerplate' ), //shows on page
                        'menu_title' => __(
'Boilerplate', 'genesis-boilerplate' ) //shows
in the menu
                )
                );

                /** Just use the defaults most
of the time other tutorials can show you how to
get advanced here */
                $page_ops = array();

                //creates the page
                $this->create(
'genesis_boilerplate_settings', $menu_ops,
$page_ops, $settings_field, $default_settings );

                //loads the sanitizer. Look for
details below.
                add_action(
'genesis_settings_sanitizer_init', array(
```

```
$this, 'sanitizer_filters' ) );

        }

        /**
         * Register each of the settings with a
sanitization filter type.
         *
         * @since 0.9.0
         *
         * @uses genesis_add_option_filter()
Assign filter to array of settings.
         *
         * @see
\Genesis_Settings_Sanitizer::add_filter() Add
sanitization filters to options.
         */
        function sanitizer_filters() {

        }

        /**
         * Loads required scripts.
         *
         * @since 0.1.0
         *
         */
        function scripts() {

        }

        /**
         * Register meta boxes.
         *
         *
```

```
    * @since 0.1.0
    *
    */
    function metaboxes() {


    }

}


new Genesis_Boilerplate_Boxes;
```

Load CSS and Javascript

The Admin section includes some details on the admin class, so I'm not going to spend much time explaining the basic class. However, since I'm encouraging readers to work on including CSS and JS, if they have come up with a good solution, I want to focus on how to do that.

I'm assuming a specific file structure with these examples. It isn't the only way to do things, but it is how I tend to build a plugin:

- genesis-boilerplate/
  - plugin.php
  - lib/
    - admin.php
    - front-page.php
    - functions.php
    - css/
      - admin.css
      - style.css

- js/

  - admin.js

  - plugin.js

If your file structure is different, you may need to amend the code used to load the Javascript and Styles.

If you are manually building your admin page, you have to build a custom action to load the styles, and you should check the page hook to make sure you are loading the scripts and styles only on your settings page. I'm going to repeat myself here:

> Only load your scripts and styles on your admin page.

I can't stress this enough. One of the biggest problems other plugins cause is when they load scripts or styles universally in the dashboard. I've even seen many plugins that are fine on their own, but they end up breaking other plugins because they've used common class names and changed them. We recently had to change our clear class because a plugin was styling .clear and gave it some strange markup. The markup probably made sense in the plugin admin page, but it broke our admin page. That should never happen. In the github issue where I fixed the issue, I said:

> To test, enable a plugin that breaks the admin screen because of stupid developers. Our classes are different and shouldn't be broken.

Please don't be a stupid developer. Make sure your scripts are loaded only on your admin page.

Fortunately, we are using the Genesis Admin Class. All you need to do is add a `scripts()` method and it will load your scripts correctly and only on your admin page. The Genesis class automatically loads this method so you do not need to use an action to load it on the right hook or check the page hook to make it load only on your admin page. This is all done automatically. You get to be a smart developer and it is super easy. That makes you some kind of dragon ninja warrior kind of developer.

So, here is the example code you can use. I've added a lot of comments to help with explaining it.

```
/**
 * Loads required scripts.
 *
 * @since 0.1.0
 *
 */
function scripts() {

        //adding some common scripts here. You
may or may not need them
        wp_enqueue_script( 'common' );
        wp_enqueue_script( 'wp-lists' );
        wp_enqueue_script( 'postbox' );

        //use wp_enqueue_script() and
wp_enqueue_style() to load scripts and styles
        wp_enqueue_script(
                'genesis-boilerplate-admin-js',
//make sure you namespace your ID and pick a
unique and descriptive name
                plugins_url( 'js/admin.js',
__FILE__ ), //adjust if needed. This
automatically builds the right URL based on the
file structure above
                array( 'jquery' ), //I'm
assuming the file needs jQuery.
                '0.1.0' //use versions so if
```

```
you have to update people get the right version
        );


        //This is enqueueing the style. It is
very similar to the script function above but
geared for styles
        wp_enqueue_style(
                'genesis-boilerplate-admin-css',
                plugins_url( 'css/admin.css',
__FILE__ ),
                array(),
                '0.1.0'
        );


}
```

Add Options

There are many ways to add options. In the Admin section, I demonstrate how to use views to add the options, but that may be a bridge to far for some people. This demonstrates an older way to add the options that is a little bit easier if you struggle with the concept of views.

The reason for building those option methods is I've found that I tend to use the exact same HTML with a few small changes over and over. It causes very long files, and that makes things difficult to read. Check out how clean the code ends up when you take time to build a method to handle repeating code.

```
/**
* Register meta boxes.
*
*
* @since 0.1.0
*
```

```
*/
function metaboxes() {

        /*
        This loads the functions that display
the boxes on the admin page.
        Make sure you use names that are unique
and descriptive.
        */
        add_meta_box(
'genesis_boilerplate_general_settings' , __(
'General' , 'boilerplate' ), array( $this,
'general' ) , $this->pagehook, 'main' );
        add_meta_box(
'genesis_boilerplate_advanced_settings', __(
'Advanced', 'boilerplate' ), array( $this,
'advanced' ), $this->pagehook, 'main' );

}

/**
 * Create General settings metabox output
 *
 *
 * @since 0.1.0
 *
 */
function general() {

        $id = 'general'; //I use an ID to link
common options together

        ?>

        <div class="wrap gb-clear">
```

```
<br />

<table class="form-table">
<!--this is using table markup to build
out the relationship for labels and options-->
<tbody>

<?php

//I created a method for building a
select field. It is clean and easy to use. Feel
free to steal and adapt it
$this->select_field( $id . '_size', __(
'Size', 'genesis-boilerplate' ), array(
        'small'  => __( 'Small' ,
'genesis-boilerplate' ),
        'medium' => __( 'Medium',
'genesis-boilerplate' ),
        'tall'   => __( 'Box' ,
'genesis-boilerplate' ),
    ) );

//I used a wrapper method here. There
were a lot of options in the full file this
plugin was for so this saved space
$this->position( $id );
//I also have another wrapper method
that automatically builds a multicheck from all
post types. Another handy thing to steal.
$this->post_type_checkbox( $id );

?>
</tbody>
</table>
```

```php
        </div>

        <?php

}

/**
 * Create Advanced settings metabox output
 *
 *
 * @since 0.1.0
 *
 */
function advanced() {

        $id = 'advanced';

        //This method builds a checkbox
        $this->checkbox( $id . '_checkbox', __(
'Enable This Option?', 'genesis-boilerplate' )
);

        //here is an example of adding a text
field directly to the screen without a method.
        ?><p>
        <label for="<?php echo
$this->get_field_id( $id . '_text' ); ?>"><?php
_e( 'Enter text here:', 'genesis-boilerplate'
); ?></label>
        <input type="text" name="<?php echo
$this->get_field_name( $id . '_text' ); ?>"
id="<?php echo $this->get_field_id( $id .
'_text' ); ?>" value="<?php echo esc_attr(
$this->get_field_value( $id . '_text' ); ?>"
size="27" />
```

```php
        </p><?php

        //an alternate solution to the abover
would be a text_field() method
        //$this->text_field( $id . '_text', __(
'Enter text here:', 'genesis-boilerplate' ) );

}

/**
 * Outputs select field to select position for
 the icon
 *
 * @since 0.1.0
 *
 * @param string $id ID base to use when
 building select box.
 *
 */
function position( $id ){

        $this->select_field( $id . '_position',
__( 'Display Position' , 'genesis-boilerplate'
), array(
                'off'            => __( 'Select
display position to enable.' ,
'genesis-boilerplate' ),
                'before_content' => __( 'Before
the Content' , 'genesis-boilerplate' ),
                'after_content'  => __( 'After
the Content' , 'genesis-boilerplate' ),
                'both'           => __( 'Before
and After the Content' , 'genesis-boilerplate'
),
        ) );
```

```php
}

/**
 * Outputs text field
 *
 * @since 0.1.0
 *
 * @param string $id ID to use when building
select box.
 * @param string $name Label text for the select
field.
 * @param array $option Array key
$option=>$title used to build select options.
 *
 */
function text_field( $id, $label ){

        printf(
                '<label
for="%s">%s</label><input type="text" name="%s"
id="%s" value="%s" size="27" />',
                $this->get_field_id( $id ),
                $label,
                $this->get_field_name( $id ),
                $this->get_field_id( $id ),
                esc_attr(
$this->get_field_value( $id )
        );

}

/**
 * Outputs select field
 *
```

```php
 * @since 0.1.0
 *
 * @param string $id ID to use when building
select box.
 * @param string $label Label text for the
select field.
 * @param array $option Array key
$option=>$title used to build select options.
 *
 */
function select_field( $id, $label, $options =
array() ){
        $current = $this->get_field_value( $id
);

        ?>
        <tr valign="top">
        <th scope="row"><label for="<?php echo
$this->get_field_id( $id ); ?>"><?php echo
$label ?></label></th>
        <td><select name="<?php echo
$this->get_field_name( $id ); ?>" class="<?php
echo 'genesis_boilerplate_' . $id; ?>"
id="<?php echo $this->get_field_id( $id ); ?>">
        <?php
        if ( ! empty( $options ) ) {
                foreach ( (array) $options as
$option => $title ) {

                        printf( '<option
value="%s"%s>%s</option>',
                                esc_attr(
$option ),
                                selected(
$current, $option, false ),
                                esc_html(
```

```php
$title )
                            );

                }
        }
        ?>
        </select></td>
        </tr><?php
}

/**
 * Outputs checkbox fields for public post types.
 *
 * @since 0.1.0
 *
 * @param string $id ID base to use when
building checkbox.
 *
 */
function post_type_checkbox( $id ){

        $post_types = get_post_types( array(
'public' => true, ) );

        printf( '<tr valign="top"><th
scope="row">%s</th>', __( 'Enable on:',
'genesis-boilerplate' ) );

        echo '<td>';

        foreach ( $post_types as $post_type ) {
                $this ->checkbox( $id . '_' .
$post_type, $post_type );
        }
```

```php
        $this->checkbox( $id . '_show_archive',
__( 'Show on Archive Pages',
'genesis-boilerplate' ) );

        echo '</td></tr>';

}

/**
 * Outputs checkbox field.
 *
 * @since 0.1.0
 *
 * @param string $id ID to use when building
checkbox.
 * @param string $label Label text for the
checkbox.
 *
 */
function checkbox( $id, $label ){
        printf(
                '<label for="%s"><input
type="checkbox" name="%s" id="%s" value="1"%s
/> %s </label> ',
                $this->get_field_id( $id ),
                $this->get_field_name( $id ),
                $this->get_field_id( $id ),
                checked(
$this->get_field_value( $id ), 1, false ),
                $label
        );
        echo '<br />';
}
```

Of course, I pulled out most of the options this file had, so there is probably a net loss or maybe a wash. With more options it can save you significant space and make it easier to change the markup on several elements at once.

Add Defaults

Once you have your options built, you should decide what the default values are.

Why bother with defaults?

If people will be setting up options, then why should you give them defaults? Remember, the goal is to make things easy for a user. If they can turn on a plugin and have it work out of the box, that is a better experience. The options page should let them set important values that cannot be decided for them or customize the feel of your plugin to quite their needs. You are the expert though, so give them a head start by providing as many default values as you can based on your experience.

Start by filling in the options that you would pick. That will give you a good idea of which values you would recommend. Now use that to fill in the defaults. This goes up in the "_construct()" method.

```
/*
If themes or other plugins should be able to
change your defaults use a filter here.
Otherwise just use the array without the filter
*/
$default_settings = apply_filters(
        'genesis_boilerplate_defaults',
        array(
                'general_size'      => 'medium',
                'general_position'  =>
'before_content',
                'general_post'      => 1,
```

```
                'advanced_checkbox' => 0,
                'advanced_text'      => __(
'Default Text', 'genesis_boilerplate' ), //if
you define default text internationalize it
         )
);
```

Sanitize Your Options

Another important step here is to sanitize the values. If you do not sanitize your content, it opens your plugin up to exploits. Sanitizing the saved option also means you can know with greater certainty what type of value will be returned on the front end of the site. The number one rule of sanitizing options is to make sure the option uses the least possible filter. A checkbox should be validated with only the possible option, typically 1 or 0. Select boxes and most text fields can be no HTML.

Fortunately, Genesis makes this very easy too. There is a class that runs various sanitization filters that you can quickly access in the Genesis Admin Class.

The example code here has those filters in what I deem to be the order of risk. If you can use a higher filter for your option, it is safer to use that filter. The lower the filter is, the more risk there is in using it.

```
/**
 * Register each of the settings with a
sanitization filter type.
 *
 * @since 0.9.0
 *
 * @uses genesis_add_option_filter() Assign
filter to array of settings.
 *
```

```php
 * @see
\Genesis_Settings_Sanitizer::add_filter() Add
sanitization filters to options.
*/
function sanitizer_filters() {

        //since I'm building some checkboxes
programatically I have to add validation
programatically.
        $one_zero = array(
                'general_post',
                'advanced_checkbox',
        );

        //this gets the post type list
        $post_types = get_post_types( array(
'public' => true, ) );

        //I add the post types to the hard
coded options so they can all be filtered
        foreach( $post_types as $post_type ) {
                $one_zero[] = 'general_' .
$post_type;
        }

        //use for checkboxes
        genesis_add_option_filter(
                'one_zero',
                $this->settings_field,
                $one_zero
        );

        //only allows integers. Great for text
fields that are just for numbers
        genesis_add_option_filter(
```

```php
                'absint',
                $this->settings_field,
                array(


                )
        );

        //used to validate a URL
        genesis_add_option_filter(
                'url',
                $this->settings_field,
                array(


                )
        );

        //if you don't NEED html in your text
field use this option for text
        genesis_add_option_filter(
                'no_html',
                $this->settings_field,
                array(
                'general_size', //these are
select fields so there shouldn't ever be HTML
                'general_position', //if HTML
shows up here someone is trying something tricky
                )
        );

        //uses wp_kses to allow some HTML but
nothing easily exploitable
        genesis_add_option_filter(
                'safe_html',
                $this->settings_field,
                array(
```

```
                'advanced_text',
                )
        );

        //allows full HTML but only for users
with unfiltered HTML priviledge
        genesis_add_option_filter(
                'requires_unfiltered_html',
                $this->settings_field,
                array(

                )
        );

}
```

CHAPTER 28

HOW TO CHANGE THE GALLERY POST FORMAT OUTPUT

For one of my recent sites, I decided to change how archives display Gallery post formats.

Previously I had the full content showing for galleries and just included a [gallery] short tag.

Mostly I like that, since people could view my images directly in the archive, but this wouldn't work well if I uploaded more than say nine images to the gallery (a 3×3 grid with my current setup). In fact, I was intentionally limiting myself on how many images I would post to a gallery because of that. When I was reading on post formats and saw how Matt Mullenweg was handling his galleries, this new approach made sense.

One of the big advantages to the Tapestry theme that I originally used on that site is the built in support for Post Formats. However, out-of-the-box it treats all post formats pretty much the same. Some of my changes added small, but key differences in the various post formats. I can now show the featured image and content limit for my standard posts, but the full content for the asides, quotes, and other formats. This change displays the featured image and content limit with text describing how many attached items are in the gallery.

Saturday April 16th, 2011 two significant storms moved through Front Royal. Neither produced tornadoes, unlike other parts of the storm system, but the rain was unlike anything I have ever experienced. At one point it looked like a waterfall with drops of water larger than a quarter. The river was already running high from several previous systems, and the creeks couldn't keep up, resulting in …

This album contains 19 items

The code for this is pretty straight forward. First, I had to adapt the Tapestry code that handles all the actions for the post formats.

```
add_action( 'genesis_before_post',
'tapestry_remove_elements' );

/**
 * If post has post format, remove the title,
post info, and post meta.
 * If post does not have post format, then it
is a default post. Add
 * title, post info, and post meta back.
 *
 * @since 1.0
 */
function tapestry_remove_elements() {

    // Setup Gallery Post Format
    if ( 'gallery' == get_post_format() && !
is_single() ) {
        remove_action( 'genesis_post_title',
'genesis_do_post_title' );
        remove_action(
'genesis_before_post_content',
'genesis_post_info' );
        remove_action(
'genesis_after_post_content',
```

```
'genesis_post_meta' );
        remove_action( 'genesis_post_content',
'genesis_do_post_content' );
        remove_action( 'genesis_post_content',
'the_content' );
        add_action( 'genesis_post_content',
'genesis_do_post_image' );
        add_action( 'genesis_post_content',
'ntg_do_gallery_post_content' );
    }

    // Remove if post has format
    elseif ( get_post_format() && ! is_single()
) {
        remove_action( 'genesis_post_title',
'genesis_do_post_title' );
        remove_action(
'genesis_before_post_content',
'genesis_post_info' );
        remove_action(
'genesis_after_post_content',
'genesis_post_meta' );
        remove_action( 'genesis_post_content',
'genesis_do_post_image' );
        remove_action( 'genesis_post_content',
'genesis_do_post_content' );
        add_action( 'genesis_post_content',
'the_content' );
        remove_action( 'genesis_post_content',
'ntg_do_gallery_post_content' );
    }

    // Add back, as post has no format
    else {
        add_action( 'genesis_post_title',
```

```
'genesis_do_post_title' );
        add_action(
'genesis_before_post_content',
'genesis_post_info' );
        add_action(
'genesis_after_post_content',
'genesis_post_meta' );
        add_action( 'genesis_post_content',
'genesis_do_post_image' );
        add_action( 'genesis_post_content',
'genesis_do_post_content' );
        remove_action( 'genesis_post_content',
'the_content' );
        remove_action( 'genesis_post_content',
'ntg_do_gallery_post_content' );
    }
}
```

If you have Tapestry you will see several differences in this code block. The special sauce for this can be found between lines 13 and 21.

Line 13 checks to see if it is working with a gallery post format and is not on a single post page.

Then lines 14-18 remove the title, post info, post meta, post content, and the_content() (this is added for other post formats since I'm showing the full content).

Line 19 adds the post image back in, since other post formats will remove that function. The real magic is line 20. This replaces the content with a new function "ntg_do_gallery_post_content()". That creates the text seen in the galleries on archives.

```
/**
 * Outputs Content for Galleries on archive
```

```
pages
 *
 *   @author Nick_theGeek
 *   @link http://designsbynickthegeek.com/
tutorials/
changing-the-gallery-post-format-output
 */
function ntg_do_gallery_post_content() {
    global $post;

    $attachments = get_children( array(
'post_parent' => $post->ID ) );
    $imgCount = count( $attachments );

    the_content_limit( 400, ' ' );

    echo '<p class="gallery-item-count">This
album contains <a href="' . get_permalink() .
'">' . $imgCount . ' items</a></p>';
}
```

Yep, that's all there is to that magic function. Anytime you work with "$post" in a function, you need to make it global (line 7).

Line 9 fetches the attachments for the post and line 10 counts how many.

Line 12 retrieves the content limit.

For standard posts I'm limiting to 500 characters, but my extra paragraph means I need a limit of 400. I've also made the link " " because I want the ellipse added to the end, but no actual link text.

Line 14 creates the last paragraph of text detailing how many images are in the gallery and linking to the post. I added a class to the `<p>` tag because I wanted to style it to align right.

GLOSSARY

A11y	Accessibility. The process and markup which makes a site accessible to all users. Considerations include but are not limited to visual impairments like inability to distinguish low contrast content, color blindness, general visual impairment, cognitive impairment that can affect interaction with and understanding of content, and other physical impairments such as muscle tremors that make fine motor controls for navigation menus with a mouse difficult to impossible. Technologies for accessibility assistance include screen readers, screen magnifiers, and keyboard interactive navigation tools. Sites with a focus on accessibility will work to make pages and content available to all users of all abilities.
Abstract	Keyword used with object oriented programing to indicate a class must be extended with the extend keyword. Additionally individual methods may be marked as abstract indicating those method must be explicitly extended in the final class. Methods and properties in subsequent classes must have the same scope and number of arguments.
Array	An array in PHP is actually an ordered map. A map is a type that associates *values* to *keys*. This type is optimized for several different uses; it can be treated as an array, list (vector), hash table (an implementation of a map), dictionary, collection, stack, queue, and probably more. As array values can be other arrays, trees and multidimensional arrays are also possible.
Child Theme	A child theme is a theme that inherits the functionality and styling of another theme, called the parent theme. Child themes are the recommended way of modifying an existing theme.
Class	A collection of code that is used to build an object. Classes have multiple components and can be defined by keywords including abstract and final.
Constants	An immutable variable. Once defined a constant can not be modified or destroyed. The value is present in all contexts after it is defined without requiring additional declaration. Constants are usually represented with all capital letters but this is not required.
CSS	Cascading Style Sheets. This is a method of generating the appearance of web elements. The rules will supersede previous rules of the same priority, which is the cascading component.

Extend	Keyword used with object oriented programing to indicate the class is using another class. The extended class may be but is not required to be abstract. Any methods or properties replaced in the class must have the same scope and arguments as the extended class. It is not required that the class extending another class be declared as final. It is possible to extend a class that is extending another class and it is possible for an abstract class to extend another class.
Final	Keyword used with object oriented programing to indicate a class can not be extended. A final class may have extended another class or it may be a complete class without extending.
Float	Type of content that represents a number with a decimal such as 1.2 or -2.45.
Function	Keyword indicating a block of code that is capable of being invoked. This may be a static function outside of a class or a method inside of a class.
Global	Keyword indicating that a variable is being used from the global scope. This variable can be originally defined outside of a function or it can be defined in another function so long as it has been applied to the global scope with the global keyword.
HTML	Hyper Text Markup Language. This is the structured markup language used on most websites to indicate the structure of the site. The w3.org organization sets standards for HTML and related languages.
HTML5	The latest version of HTML. There are several new markup tags recognized in HTML5 as well as some tags that had been recognized in previous versions that are no longer available officially. Additionally HTML5 allows for several new attributes within the tags which can further modify the way the tag is treated by browsers and screen readers.
i18n	Internationalization. The process of making code ready to localize. This involves using a special class of functions called "get text" functions for any content that is hard coded into the theme or plugin. It is also important to use text domains and to generate .pot files so translators can generate the localization files.
IDE	Integrated Development Environment. A set of tools used in the development process. An IDE is typically a single program but can be a set of programs. Tools include items like code editor, compiler, and debugger. All of the tools, whether a single program or set of programs, are accessible via a single UI.
Integer	Type of content that represents a whole number. Integers can be positive like 1, 2, 3, 4 and negative like -1, -2, -3, -4. It is possible to define an "absint" or "absolute integer" which will force positive whole numbers.
JS	JavaScript. This is a scripting language that was originally built to work in client browsers. There have been issues where code did not always work the same across browsers so libraries like jQuery were created to make the code work better cross browser and to extend the functionality of the code. In recent years JS has been extended beyond a simple client UI tool and can be used as a server level language to build web apps and a growing number of libraries exist to allow full stack development with JavaScript.
Localization	Generally, this is translating internationalized content. It can also involve converting it to another local within the same language such as from US English to UK English (British) so it is not fully correct to simple call it "translation."
Meta Box	Generally this is a collapsable and sortable container used in WordPress admin. Meta Boxes are found in admin pages and in the post/page editor. They allow for including options and other information in the WordPress dashboard.

Object	This is the interactive instance of a class. Objects can have a single use or can be used repeatedly during the course of a page load. There are several design models for using object oriented programing that makes objects very dynamic to very static.
OOP	Object Oriented Programming. A way of doing development using classes to generate objects. For more details see the Classes overview.
Parent Theme	A parent theme is any theme that is extended by a child theme. The child theme will inherit functions, markup, and potentially even scripts and styles from the parent theme. When using a parent theme, all changes should be applied via the child theme.
PHP	PHP: Hypertext Preprocessor. At one point this was an acronym for "Personal Home Page" but has grown well past that single use. PHP is a server side scripting language that builds output. It is the server level language used for WordPress and Genesis.
Private	Keyword used in object oriented programing to limit the scope of a method or property. Any method or property with the keyword private can only be accessed in the class. Any attempts to use them outside of the class will result in an error. They cannot be accessed when extending a class unless the method is added to the extending class.
Protected	Keyword used in object oriented programing to limit the scope of a method or property. Any method or property with the keyword protected can only be accessed in the object. This means they can be accessed if the class is extended but only within the object so attempts to access the method or keyword outside of the object will result in an error.
Public	Keyword used in object oriented programing to limit the scope of a method or property. Any method or property with the keyword protected can be accessed at any level including within the class, object, or outside of the object.
Schema	Special markup available in HTML (and other formats) to define the type of content being represented. This goes from very broad definitions like "webPage" to very specific types of content like "Residence."
Static	1. Keyword used in object oriented programing to indicate a method or property is available without the object. Static methods will not have access to the object, even if an object is instantiated and uses the method. Changes to static properties will affect all objects using that property. 2. Keyword used with static function to indicate the scope of the variable extends beyond the single use of the function. Static variables will retain value from one invocation of a function to the next but cannot be accessed outside of the function.
String	Type of content that represents text. This can be textual representation of integers or floats but are not integers or floats. In other words 1 == '1' but 1 !== '1'. This can be confusing so when comparing numbers it is often important to declare type to ensure values work as expected.
Theme Framework	Type of theme that creates the structure of the page and provides a set of functions and classes for modifying the structure. Generally styles and scripts are handled by the child theme while the parent theme acts as the framework. Most if not all theme frameworks are expected to be used as a parent theme.
XHTML	EXtensible HyperText Markup Language. This is a type of HTML that uses XML standards to define the structure and rules of the language. The requirements are more strict than standard HTML. This was the language used for the original Genesis and child themes prior to adopting HTML5 for the newer themes.

RESOURCES

There are so many things this book simply cannot cover. There isn't time to explain every HTML tag, PHP function or even WordPress functions. It isn't possible to go into depth for every concept touched. While I take time to cover some of the big ideas around Genesis, at some point things have to go unexplained.

That is what this resource section is for. PHP and WordPress functions used in code examples are listed with links to the official sources for those functions. Also some general references are provided for some of the big ideas touched on.

In many cases there is more than one resource listed. This may be because there is more than one official source for truth or because one resource is very technical while the other is more approachable. For example, most WordPress functions have 2 URLS provided. The older resource has "codex" in the URL and the newer resource has "developers" in the URL. The information is very similar, but not exactly the same so when possible I find it helpful to check both. However, the codex resources are being replaced with the developers resources over time, so eventually there will be a single source of truth for these resources. This is why not all WordPress functions have 2 resource URLs, in those cases the developers resource has already completely replaced the WordPress resource.

One last thing before getting into the resources, always check the comments. Many of the resources have comments with some excellent additional information.

GENERAL RESOURCES

- **Aria Attributes**

- https://developers.google.com/web/fundamentals/accessibility/semantics-aria/
- https://www.sitepoint.com/how-to-use-aria-effectively-with-html5/

- **CSS**
  - https://www.w3schools.com/css/
  - https://www.tutorialspoint.com/css/

- **DocBlock WPCS Code Standards**
  - https://make.wordpress.org/core/handbook/best-practices/inline-documentation-standards/php/

- **Genesis Plugins**
  - https://www.studiopress.com/plugins/
  - https://wordpress.org/plugins/tags/genesis/

- **HTML**
  - https://www.w3schools.com/html/
  - https://www.codecademy.com/learn/learn-html

- **i18n**
  - https://codex.wordpress.org/I18n_for_WordPress_Developers
  - https://carriedils.com/wordpress-i18n/

- **JS**
  - https://www.w3schools.com/js/
  - https://www.w3resource.com/javascript/javascript.php

- **PHP**

- https://www.w3schools.com/php/
- https://www.tutorialrepublic.com/php-tutorial/

- **Roles and Capabilities**

  - https://codex.wordpress.org/Roles_and_Capabilities

- **Schema**

  - http://schema.org/docs/gs.html
  - https://blog.kissmetrics.com/get-started-using-schema/

- **WordPress**

  - https://wordpress.org
  - http://www.wpbeginner.com/category/wp-tutorials/
  - https://learn.wordpress.com

- **WP Action Reference**

  - https://codex.wordpress.org/Plugin_API/Action_Reference

- **WP Template File Reference**

  - https://codex.wordpress.org/Templates
  - https://developer.wordpress.org/themes/basics/template-hierarchy/

- **WPCS/PHPCS**

  - https://code.tutsplus.com/tutorials/using-php-codesniffer-with-wordpress-installing-and-using-the-wordpress-rules–cms-26443
  - https://github.com/WordPress-Coding-Standards/WordPress-Coding-Standards

WORDPRESS FUNCTIONS

- __()

  - https://codex.wordpress.org/Function_Reference/_2
  - https://developer.wordpress.org/reference/

- **add_action()**

  - https://developer.wordpress.org/reference/functions/add_action/

- **add_filter()**

  - https://developer.wordpress.org/reference/functions/add_filter/

- **add_image_size()**

  - https://developer.wordpress.org/reference/functions/add_image_size/

- **apply_filters()**

  - https://developer.wordpress.org/reference/functions/apply_filters/

- **comment_form()**

  - https://codex.wordpress.org/Function_Reference/comment_form
  - https://developer.wordpress.org/reference/functions/comment_form/

- **current_filter()**

  - https://codex.wordpress.org/Function_Reference/current_filter

- https://developer.wordpress.org/reference/functions/current_filter/

- **do_action()**

  - https://developer.wordpress.org/reference/functions/do_action/

- **esc_html()**

  - https://codex.wordpress.org/Function_Reference/esc_html

  - https://developer.wordpress.org/reference/functions/esc_html/

- **get_option()**

  - https://developer.wordpress.org/reference/functions/get_option/

- **get_the_ID()**

  - https://developer.wordpress.org/reference/functions/get_the_id/

- **get_the_title()**

  - https://developer.wordpress.org/reference/functions/get_the_title/

- **is_front_page()**

  - https://codex.wordpress.org/Function_Reference/is_front_page

  - https://developer.wordpress.org/reference/functions/is_front_page/

- **is_page()**

- https://developer.wordpress.org/reference/functions/is_page/

- **is_single()**

  - https://developer.wordpress.org/reference/functions/is_single/

- **register_sidebar()**

  - https://codex.wordpress.org/Function_Reference/register_sidebar

  - https://developer.wordpress.org/reference/functions/register_sidebar/

- **remove_action()**

  - https://codex.wordpress.org/Function_Reference/remove_action

  - https://developer.wordpress.org/reference/functions/remove_action/

- **remove_filter()**

  - https://codex.wordpress.org/Function_Reference/remove_filter

  - https://developer.wordpress.org/reference/functions/remove_filter/

- **unregister_sidebar()**

  - https://codex.wordpress.org/Function_Reference/unregister_sidebar

  - https://developer.wordpress.org/reference/functions/unregister_sidebar/

- **wp_dequeue_script()**

- https://codex.wordpress.org/Function_Reference/
  wp_dequeue_script

- https://developer.wordpress.org/reference/functions/
  wp_dequeue_script/

- **wp_dequeue_style()**

  - https://codex.wordpress.org/Function_Reference/
    wp_dequeue_style

  - https://developer.wordpress.org/reference/functions/
    wp_dequeue_style/

- **wp_enqueue_script()**

  - https://developer.wordpress.org/reference/functions/
    wp_enqueue_script/

- **wp_enqueue_style()**

  - https://developer.wordpress.org/reference/functions/
    wp_enqueue_style/

- **wp_get_current_commenter()**

  - https://codex.wordpress.org/Function_Reference/
    wp_get_current_commenter

  - https://developer.wordpress.org/reference/functions/
    wp_get_current_commenter/

- **wp_kses_decode_entities()**

  - https://codex.wordpress.org/Function_Reference/
    wp_kses_decode_entities

  - https://developer.wordpress.org/reference/functions/
    wp_kses_decode_entities/

- **wp_kses()**

- ○ https://codex.wordpress.org/Function_Reference/wp_kses
- ○ https://developer.wordpress.org/reference/functions/ wp_kses/

- **wp_localize_script()**

  - ○ https://codex.wordpress.org/Function_Reference/ wp_localize_script
  - ○ https://developer.wordpress.org/reference/functions/ wp_localize_script/

- **wp_parse_args()**

  - ○ https://codex.wordpress.org/Function_Reference/ wp_parse_args
  - ○ https://developer.wordpress.org/reference/functions/ wp_parse_args/

- **wp_register_script()**

  - ○ https://developer.wordpress.org/reference/functions/ wp_register_script/

- **wp_register_style()**

  - ○ https://codex.wordpress.org/Function_Reference/ wp_register_style
  - ○ https://developer.wordpress.org/reference/functions/ wp_register_style/

- **wpautop()**

  - ○ https://codex.wordpress.org/Function_Reference/wpautop
  - ○ https://developer.wordpress.org/reference/functions/ wpautop/

PHP FUNCTIONS

- **__construct()**

  ◦ http://php.net/manual/en/language.oop5.decon.php

- **date()**

  ◦ https://secure.php.net/manual/en/function.date.php

- **define()**

  ◦ http://php.net/manual/en/function.define.php

- **preg_replace()**

  ◦ http://php.net/manual/en/function.preg-replace.php

- **str_replace()**

  ◦ https://secure.php.net/manual/en/function.str-replace.php

- **stripslashes()**

  ◦ https://secure.php.net/manual/en/function.stripslashes.php

- **unset()**

  ◦ http://php.net/manual/en/function.unset.php

MANY THANKS

One last thing. I need to thank a few people.

Thank you Brian Gardner for starting a Revolution (that is a pun on the original name of his theme company). He kicked off professional theme sales and built a great little company that became StudioPress and gave us the Genesis theme. He gave me opportunities to get involved with the Genesis community early on and eventually started paying me to do something I really enjoy.

Nathan Rice for making Genesis.

Daisy Olsen for not fearing out to much when some random guy showed up in the forums asking lots of questions then answering even more.

I'd like to list out each and every person on the old StudioPress forum support team but I'm afraid I'd forget someone so I'm going to stop there. Just know that you all taught me so very much.

I also have to thank everyone at Copyblogger/Rainmaker. You

gave me amazing opportunities to grow and I can never tell you all how much that means to me.

I also have to say thank you to the entire Genesis community. I've helped a lot of you, but you've helped me too. There is such an amazing group of individuals willing to give back and help. I honestly could not have written this book without you.

Finally, I have to thank my family. I thank my wife who put up with me doing crazy late nights when an idea wouldn't leave my head till it was finished, my kids who must think I'm surgically attached to the computer but are good at letting me work when they want to play, and my parents who got me started with a c64 when I was young and made me into the geek I am today.

Made in the USA
San Bernardino, CA
19 February 2018